This book belongs to:

....

Mrs Wordsmith ®

HOW TO WRITE
A STORY

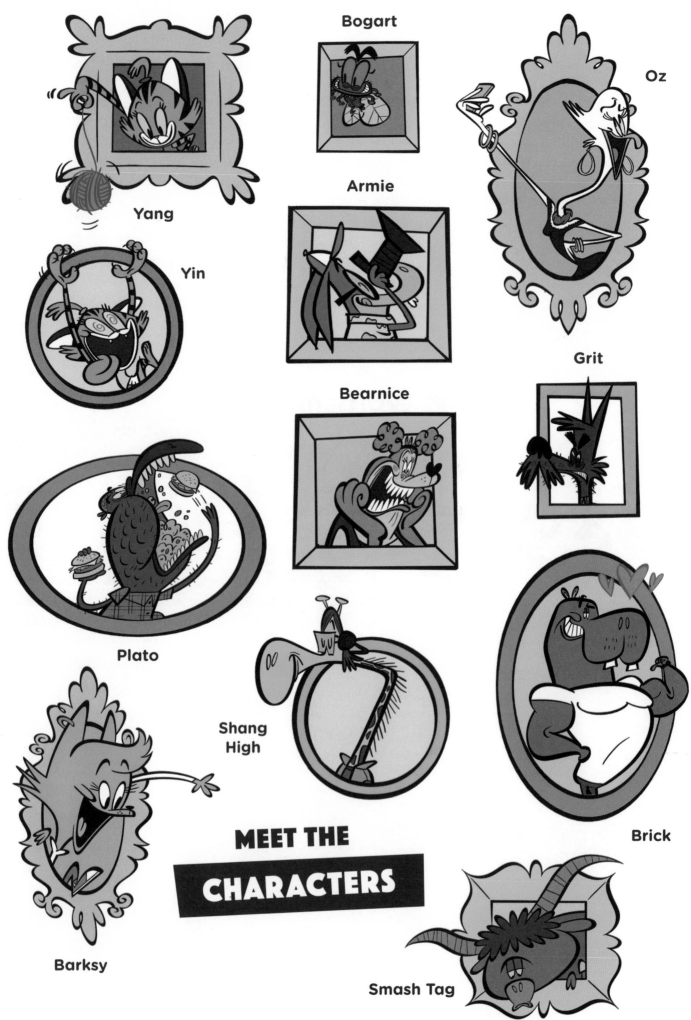

Yang

Bogart

Oz

Yin

Armie

Grit

Bearnice

Plato

Shang High

Brick

Barksy

MEET THE CHARACTERS

Smash Tag

CONTENTS

WHAT'S INSIDE?

How to Write a Story is designed to give kids everything they need to write a story on their own. It provides them with the tools, tips, and vocabulary to make it easy and fun to plan and write captivating stories that are well structured, richly descriptive, and exciting to read.

STORY SHAPES

The first section is called Story Shapes. It shows children how to create graphs to plan a character's journey, their ups and downs, and how they change from the beginning, through the middle, to the end of a story.

The graphs are illustrated to help children imagine what a good story looks like and where the different pieces fall into place. It's simple, clear, and fun.

STORY KITS

The second part includes 21 Story Kits for school or home use. They are perfect for exam prep, and they include:

• Illustrated writing prompts to fire kids' imaginations
• Targeted questions for each prompt to help kids plan their writing
• Curated vocabulary lists for each prompt to enrich kids' writing and build confidence.

MARK SCHEMES WITH CHECKLISTS

Our mark schemes are closely aligned to those used by schools and exam boards. Designed with the help of experts, this book provides further detail to let you know how stories are assessed.

USING HOW TO WRITE A STORY IN THREE SIMPLE STEPS

Step 1: Read through "Story Shapes". It's fun and beautifully illustrated.

Step 2: Keep the four Story Shape graphs in mind while preparing to write your story.

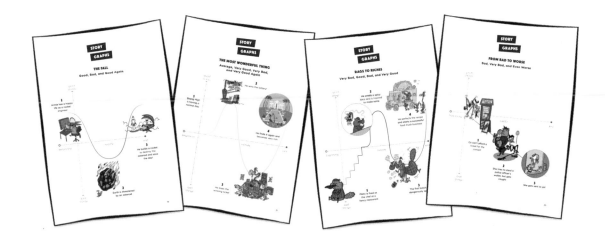

Step 3: Choose a Story Kit (illustrated writing prompt) to inspire you. It's time to get writing!

Then once you've written your story, you can simply mark it yourself!

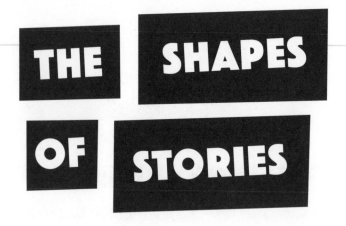

THE SHAPES OF STORIES

Stories are all about a character's journey, their ups and downs, and how they change along the way. This is what we call the shape of a story.

You're going to learn how to write a story by first learning how to graph a story. You'll learn four simple **Story Shapes** that are plotted with a **beginning, middle,** and **end** on a graph.

STORY
GRAPHS

A SIMPLE STORY GRAPH

Every story has a shape, with ups and downs
that repeat over and over again so we can
learn them by heart.

**First, let's draw a flat line. This represents time:
the beginning, middle, and end of the story.**

Your character's journey moves along this line from the
beginning, through the middle, all the way to the end.

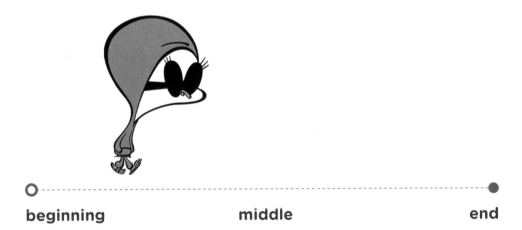

beginning   **middle**   **end**

WHAT'S WRONG WITH THIS STORY?

The character is walking in a straight, flat line.
This means nothing interesting is happening to them.
The story has no shape – no ups or downs.

For a story to take shape, it has to have more than
a beginning, a middle, and an end. Something has to
happen to your character.

STORY GRAPHS

A STORY ISN'T A STORY UNTIL SOMETHING HAPPENS TO YOUR CHARACTER

The beginning of the story is how we meet your character. The middle of the story is what happens to your character. And by the end of the story, something needs to have happened to your character that has made them change. For your story to be interesting, your character needs to change.

Beginning *how we meet your character*

Middle *what happens to your character*

End *how your character has changed*

That's why there's also an upright line on the story graph. This line is where good things and bad things happen to your character to make the story interesting.

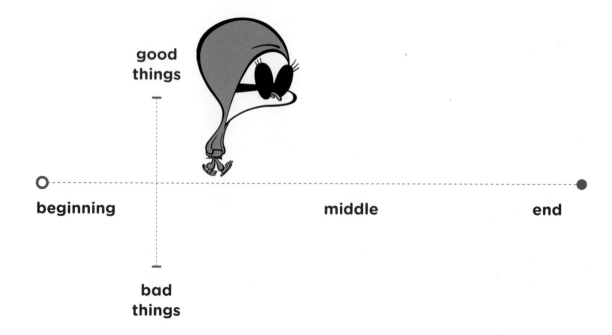

good things

bad things

beginning

middle

end

The **good** things bring the character **up** on the graph.
The **bad** things bring the character **down** on the graph.

These ups and downs create the shape of the story!

A GOOD STORY GRAPH

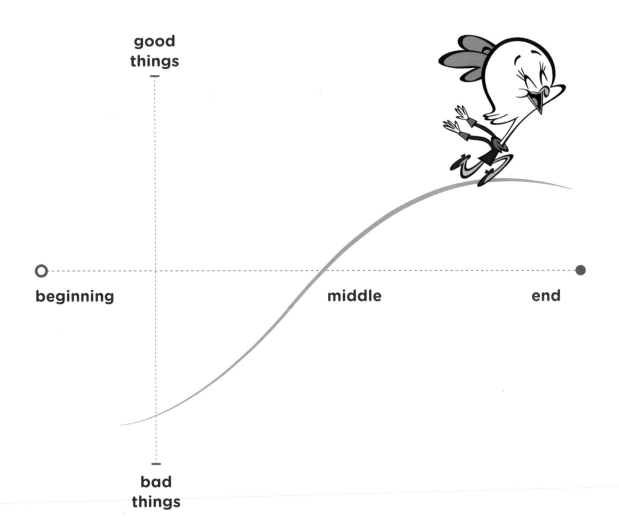

good
things

beginning   middle   end

bad
things

PLOTTING GRAPHS

HOW TO PLOT A STORY ON THE GRAPH

As your character moves along the line from the beginning, through the middle, to the end, ask yourself three questions:

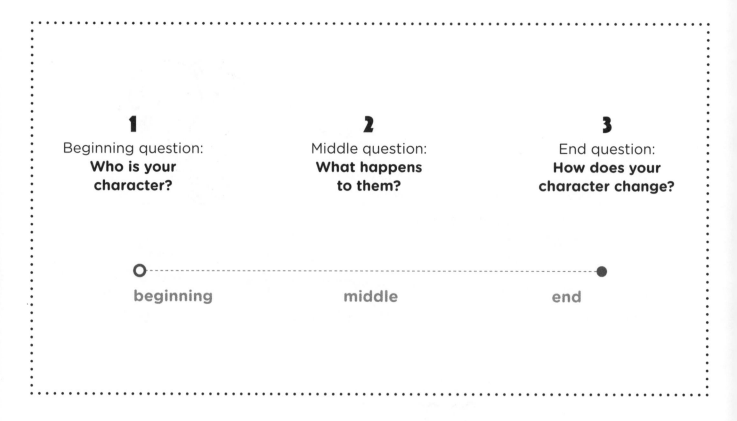

1

Beginning question:
**Who is your
character?**

2

Middle question:
**What happens
to them?**

3

End question:
**How does your
character change?**

beginning   middle   end

**These questions will provide your character with ups
and downs and give the whole story a shape.**

Beginning question:

WHO IS YOUR CHARACTER?

The opening of your story should help us get to know your character and show us everything about them. To help the reader really get a picture of your character's life at the beginning of the story, you need to describe their personality and lifestyle – but also details about where they live, what the weather is like there, and more.

Describe your character's...

- **Appearance** What do they look like? What do they wear? How do they move?

- **Personality** What is your character like, and how do they show it?

- **Feelings and needs** How is your character feeling, and what do they want more than anything else in the world?

---

good things

brave
selfless
kind

cowardly
selfish
mean

bad things

PLOTTING GRAPHS

Beginning question:

WHO IS YOUR CHARACTER?

> **Describe the setting**
>
> Describe what your character can see, hear, and smell. Where the story takes place has a huge effect on your character. Living in an enormous castle might move your character up on the graph towards good things, but living in a tiny cupboard might bring your character down.

good things

*palatial
comfortable
luxurious*

*dilapidated
modest
miserable*

bad things

2

Middle question:

WHAT HAPPENS TO YOUR CHARACTER?

This is where all the action happens. Some people call this the "build-up". It's what causes different stories to have different shapes.

"What happens to your character?" can be anything, as long as it moves your character up or down on the graph!

Here, a food-loving platypus decides to start training to win the marathon. The adventure begins!

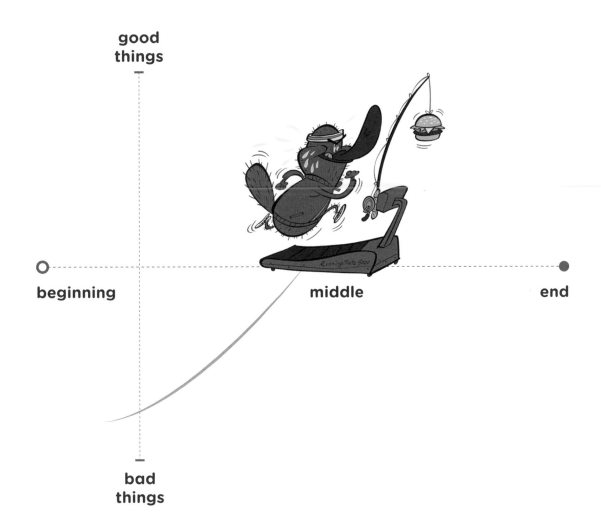

End question:

HOW DOES YOUR CHARACTER CHANGE?

At the end of any good story, the main character
isn't the same as they were at the beginning. Your
character must change when things happen to
them for the story to be interesting. The end is
where your character solves (or doesn't solve!)
whatever problems they faced in the middle of
the story. That is why the end is often
called the resolution of the story.

How did your character change?

- How did they work out their problems?
- What did they learn along the way?
- What's different about them?
- Do they become nicer or meaner?
- Do they end up better or worse off than at
  the beginning of the story?

When characters change, the shape of the story changes. That's what makes the end more exciting.

Here, our main character goes on a journey to discover her inner peace.

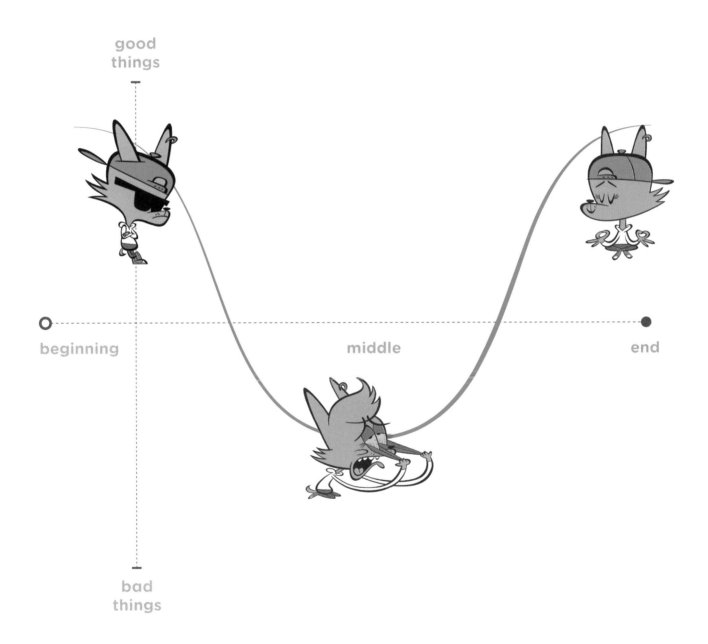

STORY

SHAPES

Let's practise understanding simple Story Shapes.
You can count on any one of these Story Shapes to
help you write a good story!

THE FALL

Good, Bad, and Good Again

GOOD

Who is your character? The character starts in a good place. A rocket engineer is enjoying doing a job he loves. Everything is great, until...

 ## BAD

What happens to them? Something bad happens. Uh oh! The Earth is threatened by an asteroid! Things are looking hopeless until...

GOOD AGAIN 3

How does the character change? The character finds a way to fix their problems. The engineer builds a rocket to destroy the asteroid and save the world!

STORY GRAPHS

THE FALL

Good, Bad, and Good Again

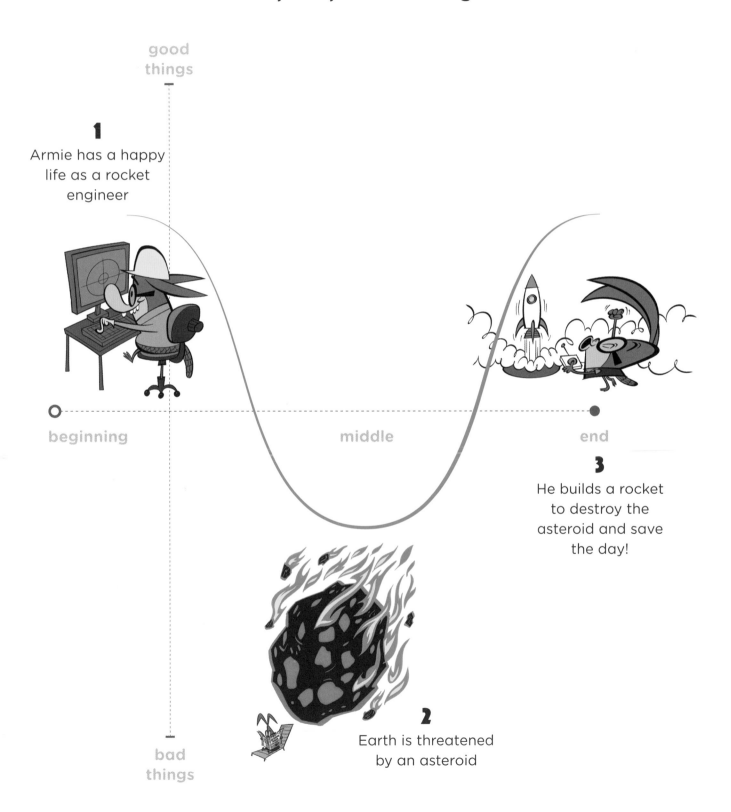

good things

1

Armie has a happy life as a rocket engineer

beginning   middle   end

3

He builds a rocket to destroy the asteroid and save the day!

2

Earth is threatened by an asteroid

bad things

19

STORY

SHAPES

THE MOST WONDERFUL THING
Average, Very Good, Very Bad, and Very Good Again

AVERAGE

Who is your character? This story starts with an average character on an average day.
A laid-back giraffe is chilling at home, listening to music. Everything is normal, until...

VERY GOOD

What happens to them? The character comes across something wonderful! Our character wins the lottery! But before long...

VERY BAD

And then what happens? The wonderful thing is lost! Oh no! Our character has somehow managed to lose the ticket before he could claim the money!

VERY GOOD AGAIN

How does your character change? The wonderful thing is found again! After lots of searching, our character finds his winning ticket. He couldn't be happier!

STORY GRAPHS

THE MOST WONDERFUL THING
Average, Very Good, Very Bad, and Very Good Again

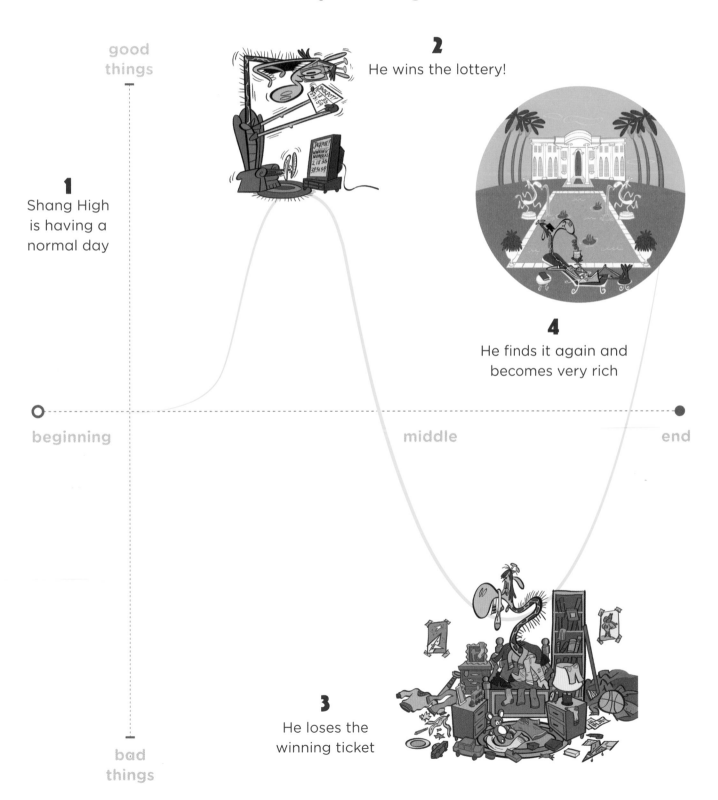

good things

2
He wins the lottery!

1
Shang High is having a normal day

4
He finds it again and becomes very rich

beginning

middle

end

3
He loses the winning ticket

bad things

RAGS TO RICHES

Very Bad, Good, Bad, and Very Good

VERY BAD

Who is your character? The character is not in a good situation. Our chef has been fired by a fancy restaurant and he's totally fallen out of love with cooking.

2 GOOD

What happens to them? But then, out of nowhere, good things start to happen. Suddenly, inspiration strikes our chef. He's going to start his own taco business!

BAD 3

And then what happens? Disaster! The tacos are dangerously spicy. They're inedible!

4 VERY GOOD

How does your character change? An unexpected lucky twist saves the day. Our chef finds a way to fix the recipe and his taco truck is a huge success.

STORY GRAPHS

RAGS TO RICHES
Very Bad, Good, Bad, and Very Good

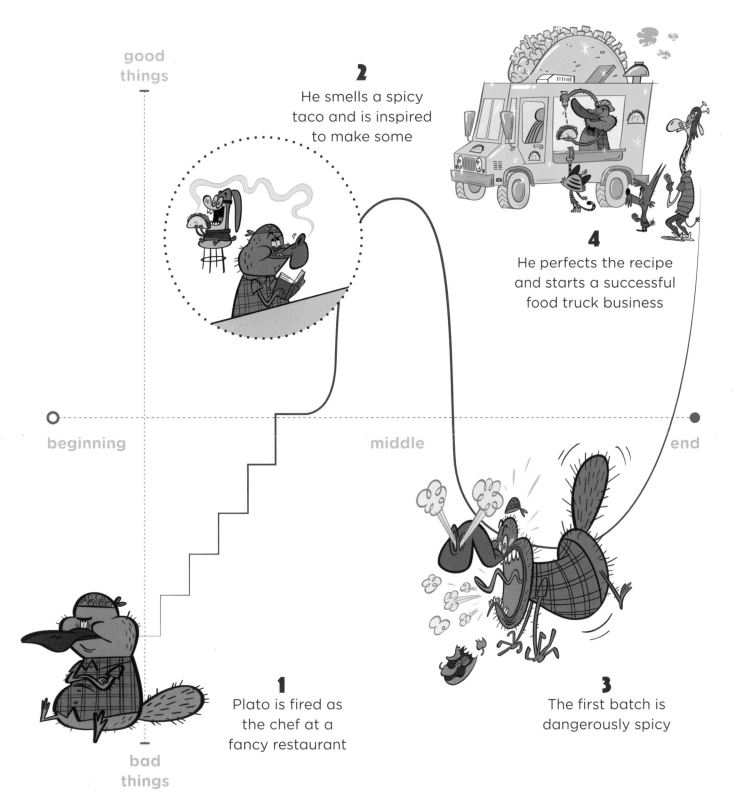

good things

2
He smells a spicy taco and is inspired to make some

4
He perfects the recipe and starts a successful food truck business

beginning

middle

end

1
Plato is fired as the chef at a fancy restaurant

3
The first batch is dangerously spicy

bad things

FROM BAD TO WORSE
Bad, Very Bad, and Even Worse

BAD   (1)

Who is your character? This story starts badly.
The character is not in a good situation. Things
are going wrong! Our character can't afford a
ticket to see her favourite band.

(2)   VERY BAD

**What happens to them? Disaster! Something
worse happens.** In desperation, our character
tries to steal a police officer's wallet to pay for
her concert ticket.

EVEN WORSE   (3)

**How does your character change? Things keep
getting worse and worse.** Our character is
arrested and sent to jail. Crime doesn't pay, Oz!

STORY
GRAPHS

FROM BAD TO WORSE
Bad, Very Bad, and Even Worse

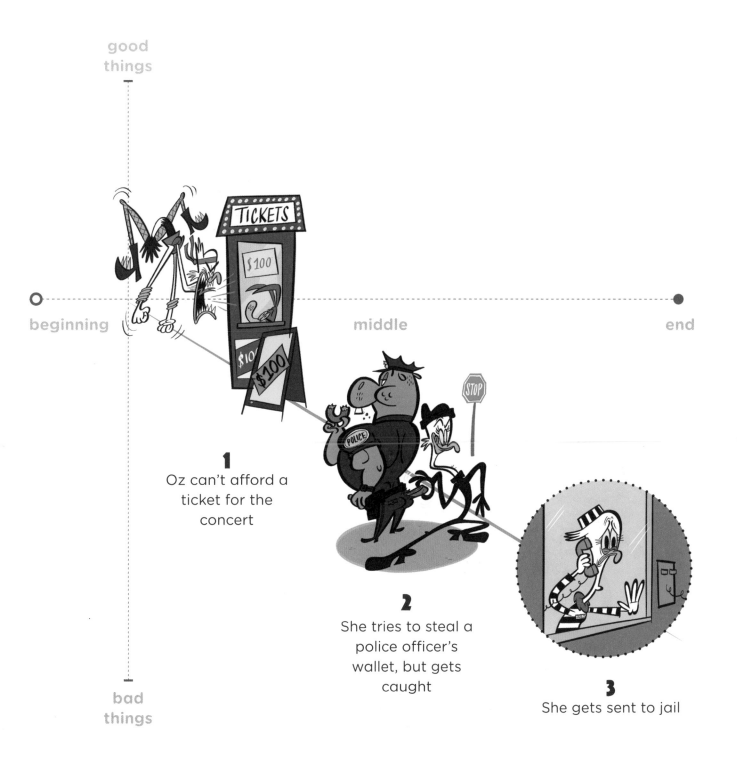

good things

beginning   middle   end

1
Oz can't afford a ticket for the concert

2
She tries to steal a police officer's wallet, but gets caught

3
She gets sent to jail

bad things

25

CHARACTERS

The key to describing a character is to show the reader what they are like in a variety of different ways. How does your character look, feel, and behave?

You want to create a picture of your character in the reader's mind. The best way to do this is to use words that **show, not tell**.

For example, if you wanted your reader to understand that your character felt angry...
This is **telling**: "Oz was angry."
This is **showing**: "Red faced and with clenched fists, Oz stormed out of the room."

Showing is far more interesting than telling!
Let's try one more example – if you wanted your reader to understand that your characters felt happy...

This is **telling**: "Yin and Yang were happy."
This is **showing**: "Yin and Yang's faces lit up as they leapt joyfully into the air."

Now let's combine this new skill with some more ideas to bring your character to life. We've split these into two categories: physical and emotional.

PHYSICAL

What does your character look like?
How does their appearance help you understand their situation? If they are wearing tattered clothes, readers will understand that they're down on their luck. Dress your character in magnificent armour, and readers will know they're a strong hero.

How does your character sound?
If their voice is fast and high-pitched, this can show that your character is overexcited. If they are droning monotonously on and on, this might show that they're dreadfully boring.

SPOTLIGHT ON...

CHARACTERS

EMOTIONAL

What motivates your character?
What do they want more than anything in the world? If they want to be rich and powerful, they might work tirelessly on a bold plan. If they feel lonely and want a friend, they might smile shyly at everyone they see.

Describe their facial expressions.
If they have wistful eyes, this might show they are kind or sad. If they have pursed lips, this might show they are stern or strict.

What is their body language?
The way your character moves and acts can be very telling. If they stand straight and tall, perhaps they feel confident and proud. If they stand hunched and avoid eye contact, this might show they feel nervous or insecure.

Showing your reader how your character physically looks, smells, and sounds, as well as their thoughts, feelings, and motivations is a great way to introduce the character!

SPOTLIGHT ON...

SETTINGS

Where the story takes place has a huge effect on your character.

If your character lives in a luxurious mansion, your reader may assume they are lucky or rich! But if your character lives in a cupboard under the stairs, your reader may assume they are unlucky or lonely.

The setting has a huge impact on the reader's first impression of your character!

There are lots of questions you can think about when describing your setting. Is it large and spacious or small and cramped? Is it indoors or outside? Once again, it's important to **show, not tell.**

Think about the setting from your character's point of view:

What can your character see?
If they see glittering golden statues and marble fireplaces, this shows they might be in a castle! If they are surrounded by tall green trees, this shows they might be in the middle of the jungle.

What can your character smell?
If they smell freshly baked cookies, this shows they might be in a bakery. If they smell something horrible and rotten, they might be in the sewers.

What can your character hear?
If they hear joyful laughter, this shows they might live in a happy home. If they hear cows mooing, this shows they might live on a farm.

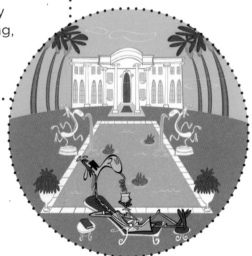

SPOTLIGHT ON...

WEATHER

Something that affects both your character and setting is the weather. The weather sets the mood for the story, so is another great way to **show, not tell.**

Think about the ways in which the weather might reflect the mood of your story:

Is it sunny?
Bright, dazzling sunshine might show the mood to be happy or hopeful.

Is it raining?
Drizzling rain might show the mood to be dreary and hopeless.

Is it stormy?
Ominous thunder and lightning might show the mood to be fearful and threatening.

SPOTLIGHT ON...

STRETCHING THE MOMENT

When you are describing something important in your story, you should build on that thought or idea with more and more detail. Don't just state what happened. Pause and take the time to describe it in detail.

Build the tension.

Streeeeeetch the moment.

The most important moment of your story might only last a second in real time, but you might want to give it longer in your writing, maybe even a whole paragraph!

We use the three sentence rule. Answer these three questions to **stretch the moment**:

• What can your character see?
• What can your character hear, taste, or smell?
• What does your character feel?

Here's an example called "The World's Spiciest Pepper":

What can your character see?
As Plato bit down into the chili pepper, his vision instantly blurred and his eyes began to water.

What can your character hear, taste, or smell?
He heard the blood pumping in his ears as the spicy taste overwhelmed him.

What does your character feel?
Sweat poured from his forehead. His mouth was on fire and his nostrils flared like industrial furnaces.

OPENING LINES

A good opening line introduces the story. A great opening line immediately draws the reader in and makes them want to read on.

Next time you open up a book, notice how the writer opens their story. Some opening lines are simple, while others are more complex. They use different tactics. Here are some of these tactics with examples from books by famous authors:

Direct address – some stories open by talking directly to "you", the reader. This can make the story feel personal, like the author knows you.

"If you are interested in happy endings, you would be better off reading some other book." *A Series of Unfortunate Events, Lemony Snicket (Daniel Handler)*

An intriguing question – this draws the reader in with an instant mystery, and the only way to solve it is to read on.

"Where's Papa going with that axe?" said Fern to her mother as they were setting the table for breakfast." *Charlotte's Web, E.B. White*

A thought-provoking statement – a short sentence with an unexpected piece of information entices the reader to want to know more.

"All children, except one, grow up." *Peter Pan, M.J. Barrie*

An emotional outburst – opening with emotive dialogue (lines in a conversation that stir up strong feelings) instantly introduces both the character and the mood of the story.

"'Christmas won't be Christmas without any presents,' grumbled Jo, lying on the rug." *Little Women, Louisa May Alcott*

A piece of history – setting the scene of your story by opening with background information is a very clear way to introduce your story.

"Mr. and Mrs. Brown first met Paddington on a railway platform. In fact, that was how he came to have such an unusual name for a bear, for Paddington was the name of the station." *Paddington, Michael Bond*

In the middle of the action – opening with something exciting happening means the reader is instantly swept up in the action.

"Lyra and her daemon moved through the darkening hall, taking care to keep to one side, out of sight of the kitchen." *The Golden Compass, Philip Pullman*

Different opening styles suit different story types, so don't be afraid to experiment!

DIALOGUE

Dialogue is a conversation between two or more characters. It is a really effective tool in story writing used to tell us more about the characters or to simply move the story forward. Here are some simple tips for using dialogue:

TIP 1

DON'T OVERUSE IT!

Too much dialogue can feel a little repetitive. It's not much fun to read a story that goes:

"Then he said... then she said... then he said... then she said..."

Remember, **show, don't tell.** Only use dialogue to **tell** us a little more about the characters, their relationship, or their actions. Then **show** us what happens next!

TIP 2

KEEP IT SIMPLE!

Dialogue is often more impactful when it's short and punchy! You don't have to write it in the same style as the rest of your story. Save your enticing metaphors (see opposite) and complex sentences for the main part of your writing.

TIP 3

THINK ABOUT PUNCTUATION!

Dialogue can be a little tricky to punctuate correctly. Pay attention to the difference between these lines:

He said, "I am sick and tired of eating green beans for dinner."

"I am sick and tired of eating green beans for dinner," he said.

TIP 4

GIVE YOUR CHARACTER A UNIQUE VOICE!

Everyone is different! If your character is a college professor they might use long, complicated words to show off their intelligence. If your character is a teenager with a viral TikTok account they might use lots of slang.

TIP 5

SAY IT OUT LOUD!

Dialogue is meant to be spoken, so the best way to check it makes sense is to read it out loud. If it sounds natural, you've done a great job!

USING WRITING DEVICES

Writing devices sound like futuristic story writing machines, but they aren't. They're actually brilliant techniques authors use to make their writing more interesting.

Using writing devices is a great way to **show, not tell** the reader something about the character, setting, or weather.

You can add depth and originality to your descriptions this way. They can be simple, or they can be wild, funny, and absurd. Have fun with them!

- **A simile** shows the similarities between two things, **using** the word "like" or "as".

  - *He devoured the sandwich <u>like</u> a ravenous wolf.*
  - *The sombre sky was <u>as</u> black <u>as</u> ink.*
  - *All the likes on her Instagram post felt <u>like</u> warm hugs.*

- **A metaphor** is a way to describe something by comparing it to something else, **without using** the word "like" or "as".

  - *The birthday party was a zoo.*
  - *Her heart was made of stone.*
  - *The video game graphics were a feast for the eyes.*

- **Personification** is when an idea or thing is described in the same way you would describe a person.

  - *The leaves danced in the wind.*
  - *The sun smiled down at me.*
  - *Fortnite wrestled me away from my book.*

- **Onomatopoeia** is when a word sounds like what it means. These words often have exclamation marks after them.

  - *Pop! Crash! Boom! Beep beep! Splash! Meow!*

VARYING SENTENCE STRUCTURE

Sentence structure is very important for effective story writing. Varying your sentences makes them more interesting! Imagine reading a story like this: "Then, she... Then, she... Then, she... Then, she...". It's a little boring to read a story in which every sentence starts the same way.

Here are a few ways you can keep your story exciting:

1

When setting the scene, you may want your sentences to be long and descriptive.

- *The tall trees cast a dark shadow as the narrow boat meandered slowly down the winding river.*

- *The music was deafeningly loud at the disco, as the bright, swirling lights entranced the dancers into a hypnotic state.*

2

When action is happening fast, you can make your sentences short and punchy.

- *She wept.*
- *The vase shattered.*

To build excitement and tension, change your sentence length from long to short.

- *The artist sprinted through the gallery, down the main hall, up the stairs, past the guards to where he had hung his priceless painting only a few hours ago. It was gone.*

- *The TikTok star watched the likes climb in her first video, from thousands, to tens of thousands, and finally spiralling into the millions. She was an overnight success.*

If you want to get your reader to think deeply or actively engage with the story, ask them a question.

- *The famous detective had solved every case she had ever put her mind to – why would this be any different?*

- *The chef was so proud to bake the traditional vanilla, royal wedding cake. "Would it be okay to make it chocolate?" he wondered.*

Mix things up with a fronted adverbial:

- *Suddenly...*
- *Beneath their feet...*
- *Beyond the snarling forest...*

Varying your sentence structure makes the story more pleasant and exciting to read and gives it a better flow!

STORY KITS

GETTING STARTED

Pick a Story Kit. Each Story Kit has:

- An exciting illustration
- Questions to help you create the Story Shape
- Lots of descriptive vocabulary and word pairs to learn and choose from

We want to make it easy for you to learn how to write a great story.

Start by writing your story in three sentences. A three-sentence story can be almost as good as a full-page story.

Answer these questions and plot them on the graph of good things and bad things.

Beginning question: Who is your character?
Middle question: What happens next? (This can include good things, bad things, or both!)
End question: How does your character change?

FIND THE RIGHT WORDS

Stories are made up of characters, settings, weather, emotions, and actions. Words will help you describe them all. Good writers use powerful words. We will give you lots of exciting words and word pairs to use.

Start by making a list of possible words. It will make your story easier to write.

WRITE LIKE A WRITER

Once you're happy with the shape of your story there are lots of ways you can upgrade your writing! Try...

- **A simile:** comparing one thing to another **using** the word **"like"** or **"as"**
  He devoured the sandwich <u>like</u> a hungry wolf.
  The sky was <u>as</u> black as ink.

- **A metaphor:** comparing one thing to another **without using** the word "like" or "as"
  The birthday party was a zoo.
  Her heart was made of stone.

- **Personification:** presenting a non-person object/concept as a person
  The leaves danced in the wind.
  The sun smiled down.

- **Onomatopoeia:** when a word sounds like what it means
  Pop! Crash! Boom! Meow! Beep! Splash!

STORYTELLING CONCLUSION

1. What journey is your character going to go on? Choose a Story Shape using the story graph.

2. Summarise your story in three sentences. Your summary doesn't have to be perfect. Just get writing!

3. Make a list of all the words you might want to use to describe the character, setting, weather, and actions in your story.

4. If you're feeling up to the challenge, try upgrading your writing with similes, metaphors, personification, or onomatopoeia!

STORY KIT 1

PROMPT

Write a story about:

being trapped in virtual reality

But first it's time to plan your story!

QUESTIONS

Who is your character?

1. How do these characters know each other? Are they friends? Siblings? Enemies?

2. What do these characters like or dislike about each other?

3. What do they look like? What are they wearing?

4. What are their personalities like? Are they clever or foolish? Generous or selfish?

5. Why do they want to enter a virtual reality? Are they excited or nervous?

What happens to them?

1. What kind of virtual reality does one of the characters enter?

2. What does it look, smell, and sound like in the virtual reality?

3. How do they get trapped there?

4. How do they feel about being trapped?

5. Do they try to escape? How? Does the other character try to help them escape?

How do they change?

1. How do the characters feel about virtual reality after this?

2. Will they try it again? How will they stop the same thing from happening?

3. Did this experience bring the characters closer together or did it tear their friendship apart?

4. What have they learned about each other?

5. What would they do differently next time?

VOCABULARY

Find the right words
Choose some word pairs, adjectives, and verbs to use in your story.

WORD PAIRS

For example: desperate escape or vivid story

experience
unique
unforgettable
surreal
eye-opening
•

simulation
simple
realistic
interactive
immersive
•

glitch
funny
major
visual
temporary
•

technology
smart
innovative
cutting-edge
outdated
•

video game
violent
classic
multiplayer
addictive
•

story
gripping
ridiculous
compelling
vivid
•

trap
sticky
devious
inescapable
diabolical
•

escape
lucky
attempted
miraculous
desperate

music
disco
electronic
epic
ambient

virtual reality
headset
bulky
wireless
noise-cancelling
malfunctioning

ADJECTIVES

realistic
true-to-life
believable
uncanny
engrossed
enthralled
absorbed
hooked
gripped
disorientated
exhilarating
tentative
wary

VERBS

play
enter
launch
fall
tumble
trip
imprison
trap
ensnare
catch
run
dodge
escape
creep
sprint
lunge
disappear
vanish
buffer
download
crash
glitch

STORY

GRAPH

Answer these questions and plot them on the graph of good things and bad things.

Beginning	Middle	End
Who is your character?	**What happens to them?**	**How do they change?**
Two twins, Carrie and Cameron	Cameron get's trapped in Carries virtual reality glasses	Become better friends

good things

What shape does your story take? Draw it here and label the parts.

○----------------------------●

beginning   **middle**   **end**

bad things

42

Write your story here!

"Mu-um!" moaned Carrie. "It's not fair! Cameron's using my VR headset again!" Cameron and Carrie were twins, born one minute apart, but they HATED eachother. It was hard enough for their mother with the divorce last month, but her twins constantly fighting was driving her even more mad. "Just let him use the dam thing! He always shares his stuff with you!" she shouted, putting her work shoes on in a hurry. "Ugh, this is so unfair," Carrie mumbled. After their mum left for work Carrie knew something wasn't right. Cameron had been using her headset last night, and he was still on it when she came downstairs that morning. Carrie tried to switch the headset off, but it didn't work. Aha! There was a button you could press that connected the headset to the tv, so ~~Carrie~~ she could see everything that Cameron was seeing. She turned the tv on after pressing the button, and....it worked! Carrie couldn't believe what

A grumpy-looking demon with deep red eyes and no hair, only shiny yellow horns. It was cackling and shouting, "Ah-ha-ha! You will NEVER escape! I will trap you here for EVER!"

MY WRITING CHECKLIST

STORY AND STRUCTURE (6/22 MARKS)

My story:

- ◯ Introduces the character – what they look like, how they feel
- ◯ Describes the setting – what the character can see and hear
- ◯ Gets the reader's attention with a clever opening
- ◯ Has a character that changes – they overcome challenges or problems
- ◯ Has a clear beginning, middle, and end
- ◯ Makes sense and sticks to the topic

LANGUAGE (6/22 MARKS)

I have used:

- ◯ **Show, not tell** (e.g. facial expressions, body language, actions, dialogue)
- ◯ Lots of colourful vocabulary that draws the reader in
- ◯ Descriptive adjectives that help the reader imagine the character and setting
- ◯ Strong verbs that show what the characters are doing
- ◯ Dialogue to bring them to life
- ◯ All past tense or all present tense throughout the story

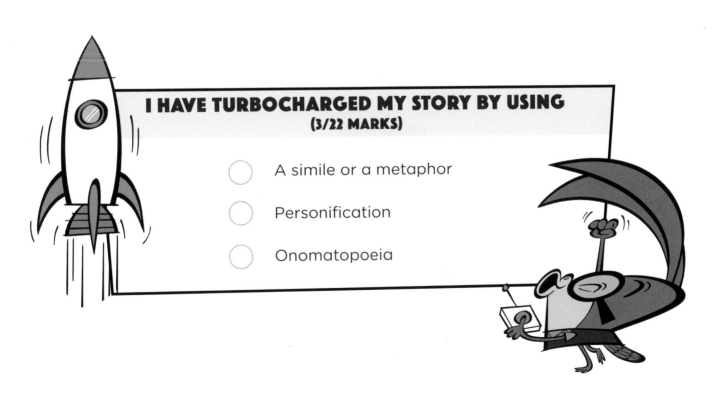

I HAVE TURBOCHARGED MY STORY BY USING
(3/22 MARKS)

- ◯ A simile or a metaphor
- ◯ Personification
- ◯ Onomatopoeia

MY WRITING CHECKLIST

SPELLING AND PUNCTUATION
(5/22 MARKS)

I have used correct punctuation and a range of sentence length to vary the pace:

○ Capital letters and full stops

○ Correct spelling

○ Question marks at the end of questions

○ Complex sentences

○ At least one short, punchy sentence

PRESENTATION
(2/22 MARKS)

My story is easy to read because it uses:

○ Neat handwriting

○ Paragraphs for each idea or part of the story

FINAL

SCORE

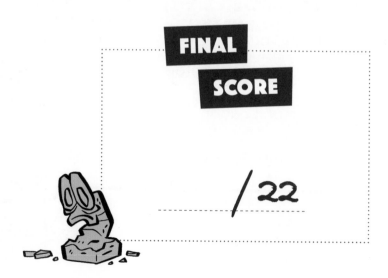

_____ / 22

STORY KIT 2

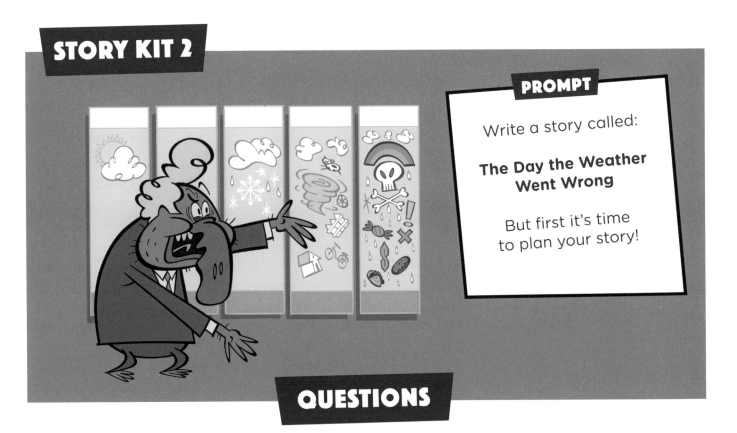

PROMPT

Write a story called:

The Day the Weather Went Wrong

But first it's time to plan your story!

QUESTIONS

Who is your character?

1. What is this weather reporter like? Are they relaxed or short-tempered?

2. What does this weather reporter look like? What do they wear on TV? How long do they take to get ready every day?

3. What is most important to them? Being famous? Predicting the weather accurately? Earning lots of money?

4. Do they get nervous before going on live TV? How do they calm their nerves?

5. What are they afraid of?

What happens to them?

1. What is unusual about the forecast today?

2. Has your character ever seen anything like this before?

3. What is predicted? Will strange things fall from the clouds? Will the wind smell like butterscotch? It could be anything!

4. Does your character give the viewers any advice? Should they stay inside? Or go out for walks and picnics?

5. How does this weather reporter feel about this unexpected change? Did they expect it or was it a surprise? Are they calm, excited, angry, or afraid?

How do they change?

1. Does the unusual weather pass? What is the world like afterwards? Does everything go back to normal?

2. How is your character's life different? Are they a hero? Does their job change?

3. Will this weird weather ever happen again? Will your character be prepared next time?

4. What lesson has the weather reporter learned?

5. What would the weather reporter do differently next time?

VOCABULARY

Find the right words
Choose some word pairs, adjectives, and verbs to use in your story.

WORD PAIRS

For example: sinking sun or fresh wind

forecast
gloomy
optimistic
ominous
changeable
•

rain
heavy
gentle
misty
torrential
•

heat
tropical
humid
sweltering
unbearable
•

presenter
popular
charming
blundering
controversial
•

wind
fresh
fierce
bitter
howling
•

ice
slippery
cracked
slushy
treacherous
•

weather
warm
extreme
unpredictable
tempestuous
•

snow
light
powdery
deep
whirling
•

object
strange
falling
unidentified
mysterious
•

sun
blazing
scorching
sinking
unforgiving
•

hail
lashing
deadly
sudden
destructive
•

darkness
complete
inky
continuous
impenetrable
•

cloud
fluffy
dense
wispy
ominous

rainbow
faint
gorgeous
vivid
magnificent

light
golden
fading
hazy
dazzling

ADJECTIVES

charming
attractive
cheerful
unexpected
astonished
shocked
tongue-tied
speechless
gobsmacked
erratic
changeable
unprecedented
unheard-of
once-in-a-
lifetime

unbelievable
incredible
miraculous
afraid
anxious
concerned
baffled
puzzled
dramatic

VERBS

fall
blow
gush
drop
pelt
describe
show
point
descend
cover
prepare
protect
hide
stare
advise
warn

Answer these questions and plot them on the graph of good things and bad things.

Beginning	Middle	End
Who is your character?	**What happens to them?**	**How do they change?**

Weather Reporter

good things

What shape does your story take? Draw it here and label the parts.

beginning ⋯⋯⋯ **middle** ⋯⋯⋯ **end**

bad things

49

MY STORY

Write your story here!

MY WRITING CHECKLIST

STORY AND STRUCTURE (6/22 MARKS)

My story:

- ○ Introduces the character – what they look like, how they feel
- ○ Describes the setting – what the character can see and hear
- ○ Gets the reader's attention with a clever opening
- ○ Has a character that changes – they overcome challenges or problems
- ○ Has a clear beginning, middle, and end
- ○ Makes sense and sticks to the topic

LANGUAGE (6/22 MARKS)

I have used:

- ○ **Show, not tell** (e.g. facial expressions, body language, actions, dialogue)
- ○ Lots of colourful vocabulary that draws the reader in
- ○ Descriptive adjectives that help the reader imagine the character and setting
- ○ Strong verbs that show what the characters are doing
- ○ Dialogue to bring them to life
- ○ All past tense or all present tense throughout the story

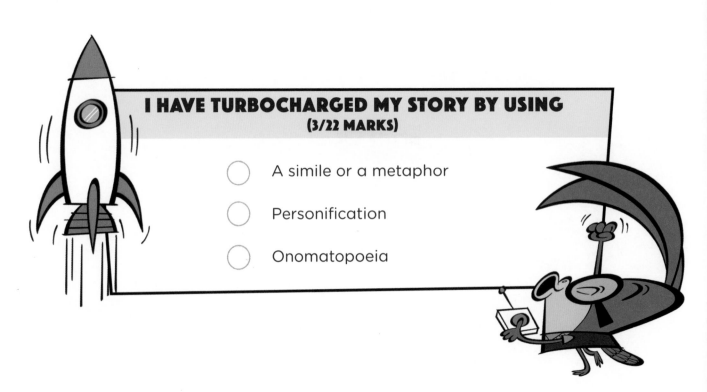

I HAVE TURBOCHARGED MY STORY BY USING
(3/22 MARKS)

- ○ A simile or a metaphor
- ○ Personification
- ○ Onomatopoeia

SPELLING AND PUNCTUATION
(5/22 MARKS)

I have used correct punctuation and a range of sentence length to vary the pace:

- ( ) Capital letters and full stops
- ( ) Correct spelling
- ( ) Question marks at the end of questions
- ( ) Complex sentences
- ( ) At least one short, punchy sentence

PRESENTATION
(2/22 MARKS)

My story is easy to read because it uses:

- ( ) Neat handwriting
- ( ) Paragraphs for each idea or part of the story

FINAL SCORE

/ 22

STORY KIT 3

QUESTIONS

Who is your character?

1. What kind of personality does your character have? Are they brave or cowardly? Mean or sociable?

2. What do they look like? What are they wearing?

3. Do they have lots of friends?

4. What are their likes and dislikes? Do they have any hobbies?

5. How do they feel about outer space?

What happens to them?

1. Why did your character move to Mars?

2. What is different about life on Mars?

3. Does anyone else already live there? Who are they? What do they look like? What language do they speak? What will they eat on Mars?

4. Does your character get lonely?

5. Will they invite more people from Earth to live on Mars with them? How will these people respond?

How do they change?

1. Will they continue to live on Mars?

2. Will they decide to fly back home?

3. What have they learned from their time on Mars?

4. What would they do differently next time?

5. Has living on Mars made them a better or worse person? Are they kinder? Or more selfish?

VOCABULARY

Find the right words
Choose some word pairs, adjectives, and verbs to use in your story.

WORD PAIRS

For example: dusty atmosphere or golden light

spaceship	**town**	**home**
gigantic	growing	comfortable
crashed	thriving	spacious
gleaming	lively	makeshift
hovering	sleepy	welcoming
•	•	•

planet	**atmosphere**	**hills**
rock	hazy	craggy
overcrowded	airless	jutting
habitable	humid	steep
deserted	dusty	low-lying
•		

light

rose-tinted

golden

dim

bright

ADJECTIVES

desolate

arid

burnt

mountainous

hazy

atmospheric

untouched

uncharted

hilly

VERBS

land

disembark

conquer

settle

discover

explore

build

STORY GRAPH

Answer these questions and plot them on the graph of good things and bad things.

Beginning	Middle	End
Who is your character?	**What happens to them?**	**How do they change?**
--------------------------	--------------------------	--------------------------
--------------------------	--------------------------	--------------------------

good things

What shape does your story take? Draw it here and label the parts.

beginning   middle   end

bad things

MY STORY

Write your story here!

MY STORY

MY WRITING CHECKLIST

STORY AND STRUCTURE (6/22 MARKS)

My story:

○ Introduces the character – what they look like, how they feel

○ Describes the setting – what the character can see and hear

○ Gets the reader's attention with a clever opening

○ Has a character that changes – they overcome challenges or problems

○ Has a clear beginning, middle, and end

○ Makes sense and sticks to the topic

LANGUAGE (6/22 MARKS)

I have used:

○ **Show, not tell** (e.g. facial expressions, body language, actions, dialogue)

○ Lots of colourful vocabulary that draws the reader in

○ Descriptive adjectives that help the reader imagine the character and setting

○ Strong verbs that show what the characters are doing

○ Dialogue to bring them to life

○ All past tense or all present tense throughout the story

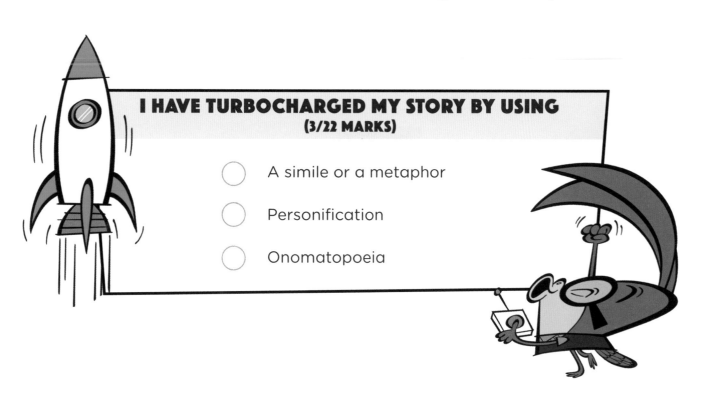

I HAVE TURBOCHARGED MY STORY BY USING
(3/22 MARKS)

○ A simile or a metaphor

○ Personification

○ Onomatopoeia

MY WRITING CHECKLIST

SPELLING AND PUNCTUATION
(5/22 MARKS)

I have used correct punctuation and a range of sentence length to vary the pace:

- ◯ Capital letters and full stops
- ◯ Correct spelling
- ◯ Question marks at the end of questions
- ◯ Complex sentences
- ◯ At least one short, punchy sentence

PRESENTATION
(2/22 MARKS)

My story is easy to read because it uses:

- ◯ Neat handwriting
- ◯ Paragraphs for each idea or part of the story

FINAL SCORE

_____ / 22

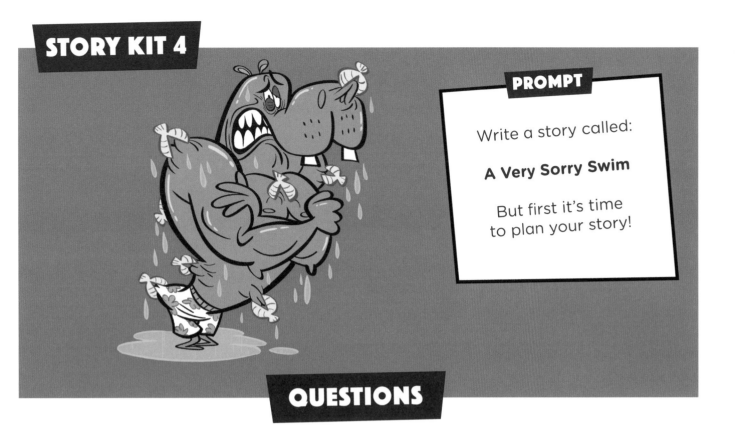

STORY KIT 4

PROMPT

Write a story called:

A Very Sorry Swim

But first it's time to plan your story!

QUESTIONS

Who is your character?

1. What is your character like as a person?

2. Are they brave or cowardly? Clever or foolish?

3. How physically fit are they? Are they very muscly? Do they move gracefully?

4. Do they usually enjoy swimming? How often do they do it? Are they very good at it?

5. What do they wear to go swimming?

What happens to them?

1. Where did they go swimming this time?

2. How long were they swimming for?

3. Why did they go swimming?

4. How do they feel physically? Was it painful? Or exhausting? Freezing?

5. What happened while they were swimming? Was it dangerous? Uncomfortable? Frightening?

How do they change?

1. How did your character recover?

2. Did they learn anything new?

3. How will they make themselves feel better? A warm bath? A hot chocolate?

4. Will they ever go swimming again?

5. What would your character do differently next time?

VOCABULARY

Find the right words
Choose some word pairs, adjectives,
and verbs to use in your story.

WORD PAIRS

For example: deep sea or crashing waves

water	**seaweed**	**swimsuit**
deep	slimy	gorgeous
shallow	floating	uncomfortable
murky	tangled	tight-fitting
choppy	invasive	loose-fitting
•	•	•
rocks	**sand**	**waves**
sharp	golden	crashing
slippery	coarse	enormous
jagged	caked	foamy
submerged	pristine	surging

ADJECTIVES

freezing
icy
lukewarm
tepid
salty
stinging
tumultuous
sticky
tangled
rough
wild
solitary
worried
sore
painful
exhausted
worn-out
washed-up

VERBS

swim
paddle
splash
dive
plunge
submerge
drift
float
bob
pinch
snag
catch
graze
bruise
attach
wriggle
thrash
gasp
swallow
panic

STORY

GRAPH

Answer these questions and plot them on the graph of good things and bad things.

Beginning	Middle	End
Who is your character?	**What happens to them?**	**How do they change?**

------------------------------   ------------------------------   ------------------------------

------------------------------   ------------------------------   ------------------------------

good things

What shape does your story take? Draw it here and label the parts.

beginning   **middle**   **end**

bad things

MY STORY

Write your story here!

MY WRITING CHECKLIST

STORY AND STRUCTURE (6/22 MARKS)

My story:

○ Introduces the character – what they look like, how they feel

○ Describes the setting – what the character can see and hear

○ Gets the reader's attention with a clever opening

○ Has a character that changes – they overcome challenges or problems

○ Has a clear beginning, middle, and end

○ Makes sense and sticks to the topic

LANGUAGE (6/22 MARKS)

I have used:

○ **Show, not tell** (e.g. facial expressions, body language, actions, dialogue)

○ Lots of colourful vocabulary that draws the reader in

○ Descriptive adjectives that help the reader imagine the character and setting

○ Strong verbs that show what the characters are doing

○ Dialogue to bring them to life

○ All past tense or all present tense throughout the story

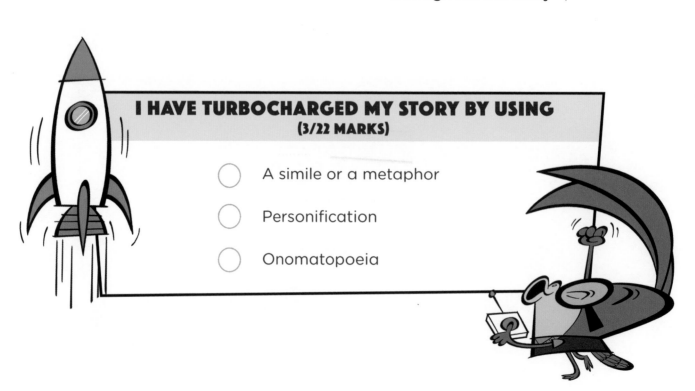

I HAVE TURBOCHARGED MY STORY BY USING
(3/22 MARKS)

○ A simile or a metaphor

○ Personification

○ Onomatopoeia

SPELLING AND PUNCTUATION
(5/22 MARKS)

I have used correct punctuation and a range of sentence length to vary the pace:

○ Capital letters and full stops

○ Correct spelling

○ Question marks at the end of questions

○ Complex sentences

○ At least one short, punchy sentence

PRESENTATION
(2/22 MARKS)

My story is easy to read because it uses:

○ Neat handwriting

○ Paragraphs for each idea or part of the story

FINAL SCORE

_____ / 22

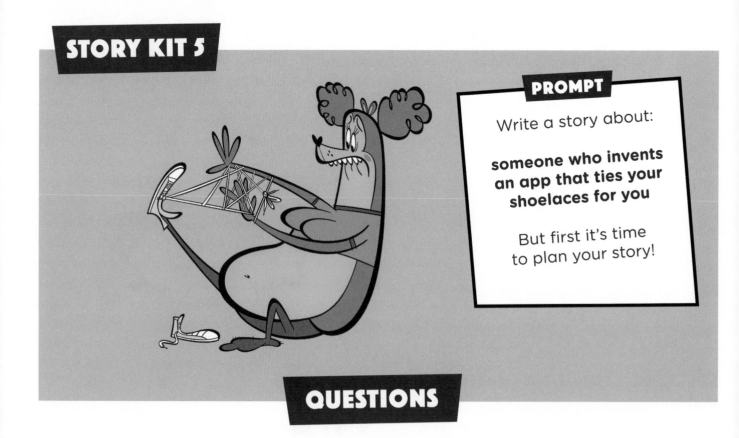

STORY KIT 5

PROMPT

Write a story about:

someone who invents an app that ties your shoelaces for you

But first it's time to plan your story!

QUESTIONS

Who is your character?

1. What kind of personality does your character have? Are they clever or foolish?

2. Do they have lots of friends?

3. What motivates them?

4. Have they invented apps before? What did they do?

5. Do they know how to tie their shoes? If not, why?

What happens to them?

1. What made them want to invent this app?

2. What tests did the character need to run to make sure the app worked correctly?

3. How does the character feel about creating the app? Are they proud or upset?

4. Is the app successful? Do lots of people use it? Or nobody?

5. What would happen if everyone in the world downloaded this shoelace-tying app?

How do they change?

1. What lesson does the character learn?

2. What would they do differently next time?

3. Do they ever learn to tie their shoelaces without the app?

4. Does this experience change their outlook?

5. What app will this character invent next?

VOCABULARY

WORD PAIRS

For example: useless app or iconic shoes

idea	**sidekick**	**expertise**
radical	trusty	relevant
innovative	loveable	technical
controversial	reluctant	unparalleled
abstract	sycophantic	invaluable
•	•	•
teamwork	**shoelaces**	**shoes**
tense	loose	high-top
solid	dangling	slip-on
exemplary	straggling	iconic
collaborative	frayed	lightweight
•	•	•
app	**coder**	**challenge**
useless	talented	tough
intuitive	experienced	daunting
nifty	budding	logistical
interactive	amateur	insurmountable

ADJECTIVES

renegade
simple
basic
essential
handy
helpful
productive
constructive
user-friendly
informative
convoluted
bewildering
perplexing
tangled
knotted

VERBS

brainstorm
solve
code
programme
design
innovate
invent
research
focus
concentrate
upgrade
collaborate
cooperate

STORY

GRAPH

Answer these questions and plot them on the graph of good things and bad things.

Beginning	Middle	End
Who is your character?	**What happens to them?**	**How do they change?**
-------------------------------	-------------------------------	-------------------------------
-------------------------------	-------------------------------	-------------------------------

good things

What shape does your story take? Draw it here and label the parts.

beginning   middle   end

bad things

MY STORY

Write your story here!

MY
STORY

MY WRITING CHECKLIST

STORY AND STRUCTURE (6/22 MARKS)

My story:

○ Introduces the character – what they look like, how they feel

○ Describes the setting – what the character can see and hear

○ Gets the reader's attention with a clever opening

○ Has a character that changes – they overcome challenges or problems

○ Has a clear beginning, middle, and end

○ Makes sense and sticks to the topic

LANGUAGE (6/22 MARKS)

I have used:

○ **Show, not tell** (e.g. facial expressions, body language, actions, dialogue)

○ Lots of colourful vocabulary that draws the reader in

○ Descriptive adjectives that help the reader imagine the character and setting

○ Strong verbs that show what the characters are doing

○ Dialogue to bring them to life

○ All past tense or all present tense throughout the story

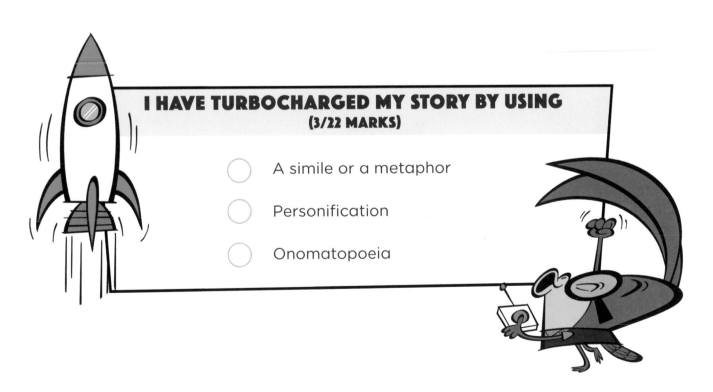

I HAVE TURBOCHARGED MY STORY BY USING (3/22 MARKS)

○ A simile or a metaphor

○ Personification

○ Onomatopoeia

MY WRITING CHECKLIST

SPELLING AND PUNCTUATION
(5/22 MARKS)

I have used correct punctuation and a range of sentence length to vary the pace:

◯ Capital letters and full stops

◯ Correct spelling

◯ Question marks at the end of questions

◯ Complex sentences

◯ At least one short, punchy sentence

PRESENTATION
(2/22 MARKS)

My story is easy to read because it uses:

◯ Neat handwriting

◯ Paragraphs for each idea or part of the story

FINAL
SCORE

_____ / 22

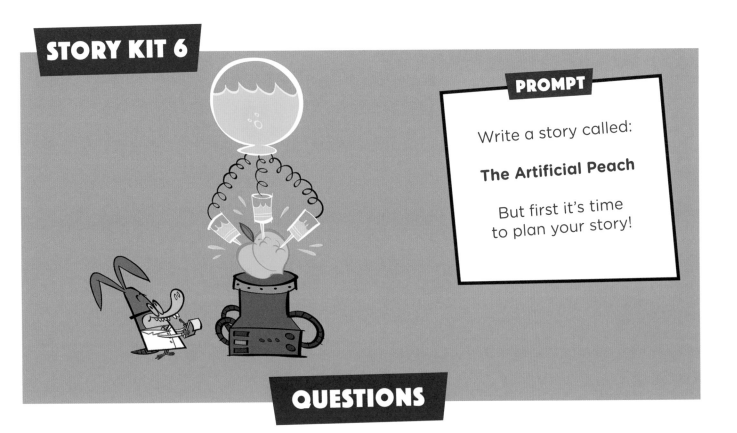

STORY KIT 6

PROMPT

Write a story called:

The Artificial Peach

But first it's time
to plan your story!

QUESTIONS

Who is your character?

1. Is your character a scientist? Is there a particular kind of science they are interested in?

2. What was their proudest invention until now?

3. What kind of person are they? Are they generous or greedy? Are they clever or foolish?

4. What does your character look like? What do they wear at work?

5. What made them want to create a peach? Why is this important to them?

What happens to them?

1. Where did your character create this peach? In a secret laboratory? What does that look like?

2. Did anyone help your character? Did anyone try to sabotage them?

3. What kind of scientific equipment did they use?

4. What happens during the experiment? Does the peach ever stop growing? Does it explode? Does it turn a strange purple or green?

5. What does the peach taste like?

How do they change?

1. Are they happy with the way the peach turned out? Are they proud or disappointed?

2. What will the character do with their invention?

3. What will the character invent next?

4. What lesson has the character learned?

5. What would the character do differently next time?

VOCABULARY

Find the right words

Choose some word pairs, adjectives, and verbs to use in your story.

WORD PAIRS

For example: artificial flavour or unique invention

scientist	**flavour**	**juice**
famous	strong	fresh
leading	unusual	sweet
prominent	intense	bitter
eccentric	artificial	acidic
•	•	•

experiment	**peach**	**machine**
dangerous	plump	robotic
top-secret	mushy	industrial
successful	sour	marvellous
innovative	succulent	sophisticated
•	•	•

laboratory	**fruit**	**invention**
state-of-the-art	ripe	important
high-security	tropical	ingenious
top-secret	sour	unique
underground	organic	ludicrous

ADJECTIVES

renegade

innovative

rebellious

unstoppable

modify

proud

audacious

pointless

daft

foolish

inexplicable

fake

artificial

VERBS

swell

inject

pump

announce

present

sell

earn

imitate

copy

create

STORY

GRAPH

Answer these questions and plot them on the graph of good things and bad things.

Beginning	Middle	End
Who is your character?	**What happens to them?**	**How do they change?**

-------------------------------- | -------------------------------- | --------------------------------

-------------------------------- | -------------------------------- | --------------------------------

good things

What shape does your story take? Draw it here and label the parts.

beginning   **middle**   **end**

bad things

MY STORY

Write your story here!

MY WRITING CHECKLIST

STORY AND STRUCTURE (6/22 MARKS)

My story:

- ◯ Introduces the character – what they look like, how they feel
- ◯ Describes the setting – what the character can see and hear
- ◯ Gets the reader's attention with a clever opening
- ◯ Has a character that changes – they overcome challenges or problems
- ◯ Has a clear beginning, middle, and end
- ◯ Makes sense and sticks to the topic

LANGUAGE (6/22 MARKS)

I have used:

- ◯ **Show, not tell** (e.g. facial expressions, body language, actions, dialogue)
- ◯ Lots of colourful vocabulary that draws the reader in
- ◯ Descriptive adjectives that help the reader imagine the character and setting
- ◯ Strong verbs that show what the characters are doing
- ◯ Dialogue to bring them to life
- ◯ All past tense or all present tense throughout the story

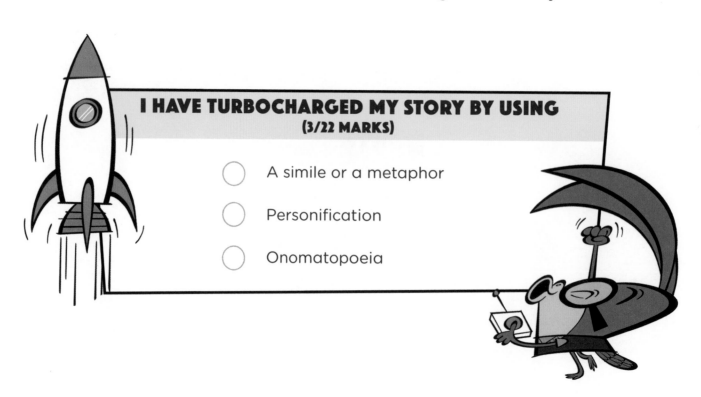

I HAVE TURBOCHARGED MY STORY BY USING
(3/22 MARKS)

- ◯ A simile or a metaphor
- ◯ Personification
- ◯ Onomatopoeia

SPELLING AND PUNCTUATION
(5/22 MARKS)

I have used correct punctuation and a range of sentence length to vary the pace:

○ Capital letters and full stops

○ Correct spelling

○ Question marks at the end of questions

○ Complex sentences

○ At least one short, punchy sentence

PRESENTATION
(2/22 MARKS)

My story is easy to read because it uses:

○ Neat handwriting

○ Paragraphs for each idea or part of the story

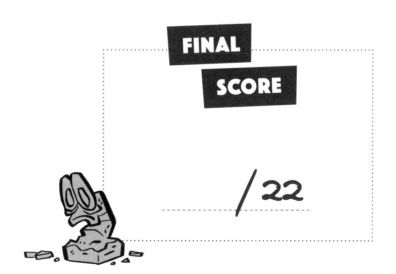

FINAL

SCORE

_____ / 22

QUESTIONS

Who is your character?

1. Who is following this pie?

2. What do they look like?

3. What is their favourite pie flavour? Sweet, savoury, or spicy?

4. Why are they following the pie?

5. What kind of person are they?

What happens to them?

1. Who baked the pie? How does the pie smell? How does it taste?

2. What went into it? Does it have any unusual ingredients?

3. What effect does the smell have on your character? What is dangerous about the pie? Is it magical? Is it hypnotic?

4. Where does the pie lead your character? Is the location close or far away from home? Is it safe or dangerous?

5. How long do they follow the pie for? How long are they under the pie's spell for?

How do they change?

1. What happens to them? Are they transformed into something else? Are they sick? Do they suddenly have magical powers?

2. Does your character escape from the dangerously delicious pie? How?

3. How does your character feel about the pie at the end of the story?

4. What lesson has the character learned?

5. What would the character do differently next time?

VOCABULARY

WORD PAIRS

For example: burnt crust or lucky spell

pie	**ingredient**	**spell**
traditional	essential	lucky
homemade	secret	sleeping
scrumptious	harmful	hypnotic
oven-fresh	pungent	potent
•	•	•
pastry	**recipe**	**curse**
flaky	original	dark
buttery	basic	evil
crumbly	age-old	terrible
delicate	treasured	ancient
•	•	•
crust	**trance**	**filling**
crisp	deep	sweet
burnt	sudden	savoury
golden	dreamy	runny
flaky	mesmeric	luscious

ADJECTIVES

visionary

magical

unearthly

supernatural

mysterious

eerie

powerful

intense

pungent

acrid

penetrating

faint

fruity

savoury

spicy

peppery

caramelised

sugary

buttery

golden

VERBS

mix

bake

prepare

roast

develop

create

sniff

STORY GRAPH

Answer these questions and plot them on the graph of good things and bad things.

Beginning	Middle	End
Who is your character?	**What happens to them?**	**How do they change?**
-----------	-----------	-----------
-----------	-----------	-----------

good things

What shape does your story take? Draw it here and label the parts.

beginning   middle   end

bad things

MY STORY

Write your story here!

MY STORY

MY WRITING CHECKLIST

STORY AND STRUCTURE (6/22 MARKS)

My story:

- ◯ Introduces the character – what they look like, how they feel
- ◯ Describes the setting – what the character can see and hear
- ◯ Gets the reader's attention with a clever opening
- ◯ Has a character that changes – they overcome challenges or problems
- ◯ Has a clear beginning, middle, and end
- ◯ Makes sense and sticks to the topic

LANGUAGE (6/22 MARKS)

I have used:

- ◯ **Show, not tell** (e.g. facial expressions, body language, actions, dialogue)
- ◯ Lots of colourful vocabulary that draws the reader in
- ◯ Descriptive adjectives that help the reader imagine the character and setting
- ◯ Strong verbs that show what the characters are doing
- ◯ Dialogue to bring them to life
- ◯ All past tense or all present tense throughout the story

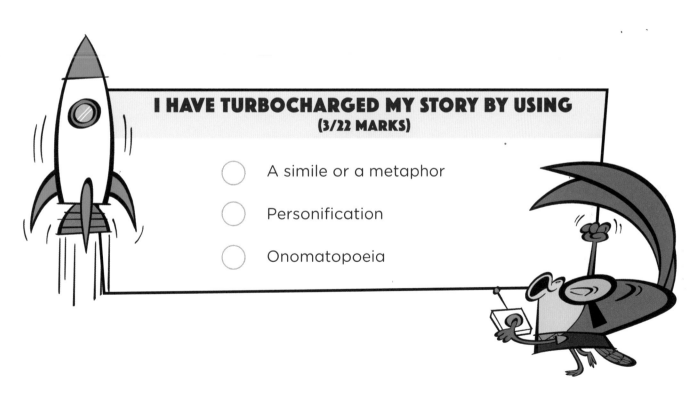

I HAVE TURBOCHARGED MY STORY BY USING
(3/22 MARKS)

- ◯ A simile or a metaphor
- ◯ Personification
- ◯ Onomatopoeia

MY WRITING CHECKLIST

SPELLING AND PUNCTUATION
(5/22 MARKS)

I have used correct punctuation and a range of sentence length to vary the pace:

○ Capital letters and full stops

○ Correct spelling

○ Question marks at the end of questions

○ Complex sentences

○ At least one short, punchy sentence

PRESENTATION
(2/22 MARKS)

My story is easy to read because it uses:

○ Neat handwriting

○ Paragraphs for each idea or part of the story

FINAL

SCORE

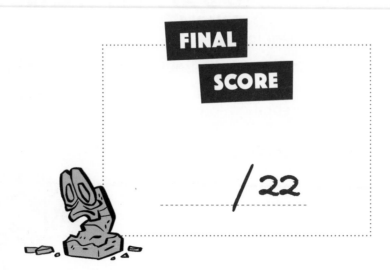

_____ / 22

PROMPT

Write a story called:

The Unbreakable Bread

But first it's time to plan your story!

QUESTIONS

Who is your character?

1. Who is the character trying to break the unbreakable bread?

2. What is their job? Are they a teacher? A scientist? A chef?

3. What is their personality like? Are they clever or foolish?

4. What do they look like? What are they wearing?

5. Where do they try to break the unbreakable bread? Are they at home or in a laboratory?

What happens to them?

1. Where did the bread come from? Do they know who baked it?

2. Why are they trying so hard to break the bread?

3. How do they feel about not being able to break the bread?

4. What is the bread made of that makes it unbreakable?

5. Will they manage to do it? What will they do with the bread if/when they do break it? How will they celebrate?

How do they change?

1. What lesson does the character learn from trying to break into this bread?

2. What kind of challenge will they take on next? What are their hopes for the future?

3. How does your character's personality change after this?

4. What lesson has the character learned?

5. What would the character do differently next time?

VOCABULARY

Find the right words
Choose some word pairs, adjectives,
and verbs to use in your story.

WORD PAIRS

For example: plastic knife or powerful tools

bread	**hammer**	**saw**
fresh	giant	electric
crusty	heavy	double-edged
stale	mighty	multi-blade
sliced	gigantic	serrated
•	•	•
knife	**tools**	**drill**
plastic	powerful	handheld
blunt	effective	high-speed
rusty	automated	deafening
razor-sharp	versatile	out-of-control
•		
goggles		
protective		
bulky		
foggy		
magnifying		

ADJECTIVES

mighty

weighty

rock-hard

concrete

solid

dense

crusty

stale

robust

sturdy

brutal

destructive

violent

electric

chemical

blunt

sharp

high-speed

VERBS

swing

slam

whack

slice

bounce

bump

bruise

drop

throw

smash

STORY

GRAPH

Answer these questions and plot them on the graph of good things and bad things.

Beginning	Middle	End
Who is your character?	**What happens to them?**	**How do they change?**

- -

- -

 **good things**

What shape does your story take? Draw it here and label the parts.

beginning　　　　　　**middle**　　　　　　**end**

bad things

MY STORY

Write your story here!

MY WRITING CHECKLIST

STORY AND STRUCTURE (6/22 MARKS)

My story:

- ◯ Introduces the character – what they look like, how they feel
- ◯ Describes the setting – what the character can see and hear
- ◯ Gets the reader's attention with a clever opening
- ◯ Has a character that changes – they overcome challenges or problems
- ◯ Has a clear beginning, middle, and end
- ◯ Makes sense and sticks to the topic

LANGUAGE (6/22 MARKS)

I have used:

- ◯ **Show, not tell** (e.g. facial expressions, body language, actions, dialogue)
- ◯ Lots of colourful vocabulary that draws the reader in
- ◯ Descriptive adjectives that help the reader imagine the character and setting
- ◯ Strong verbs that show what the characters are doing
- ◯ Dialogue to bring them to life
- ◯ All past tense or all present tense throughout the story

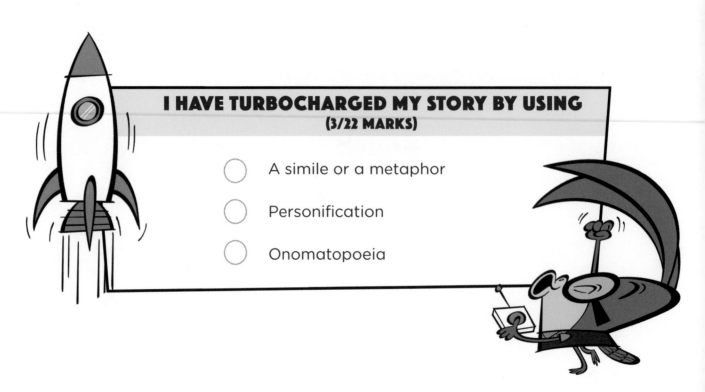

I HAVE TURBOCHARGED MY STORY BY USING (3/22 MARKS)

- ◯ A simile or a metaphor
- ◯ Personification
- ◯ Onomatopoeia

SPELLING AND PUNCTUATION
(5/55 MARKS)

I have used correct punctuation and a range of sentence length to vary the pace:

○ Capital letters and full stops

○ Correct spelling

○ Question marks at the end of questions

○ Complex sentences

○ At least one short, punchy sentence

PRESENTATION
(2/22 MARKS)

My story is easy to read because it uses:

○ Neat handwriting

○ Paragraphs for each idea or part of the story

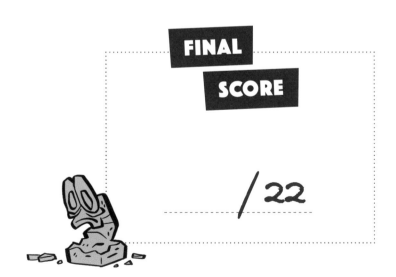

FINAL SCORE

_____ / 22

PROMPT

Write a story called:

**The Worst
Job Interview Ever**

But first it's time
to plan your story!

QUESTIONS

Who is your character?

1. Who is the character standing in front of the skyscraper?

2. What is their personality like? Are they generous or selfish? Are they clever or foolish?

3. What are they really good at?

4. What is the most annoying thing about them?

5. What is the character wearing? Are their clothes formal or casual?

What happens to them?

1. What is inside the skyscraper? Is it an office? What kind?

2. Why is the character outside the skyscraper? Do they dream of working there? What's the job?

3. What emotions does the character feel standing in front of the tall building?

4. What happens when the character enters the building? Do they have an interview? What questions are they asked?

5. Does anything go wrong? Or does everything go according to plan?

How do they change?

1. What lesson has the character learned from their experience?

2. Does the character get their dream job?

3. How does their outlook change because of their experience?

4. What kind of challenge will they take on next? What are their hopes for the future?

5. What would the character do differently next time?

VOCABULARY

Find the right words

Choose some word pairs, adjectives, and verbs to use in your story.

WORD PAIRS

For example: fake smile or well-paid job

suit
tailored
chic
expensive
hand-me-down
•

handshake
confident
limp
awkward
bone-crushing
•

interview
lengthy
informal
embarrassing
gruelling
•

shoes
classy
scuffed
stylish
designer
•

skyscraper
glinting
towering
prominent
intimidating
•

questions
silly
tough
obvious
philosophical
•

coat
faded
fur-lined
sleek
threadbare
•

office
formal
dingy
spacious
air-conditioned

job
stressful
well-paid
demanding
rewarding

smile
fake
welcoming
charming
infectious

ADJECTIVES

hesitant
nervous
uncertain
insecure
bashful
confident
self-assured
cool-headed
polite
charming
phlegmatic
impressive
imposing
intimidating
grand
magnificent
fashionable
ultra-modern
flashy
sophisticated
awkward
embarrassing
tense
cringeworthy

VERBS

dither
hesitate
pause
wait
greet
meet
smile
grin

Answer these questions and plot them on the graph of good things and bad things.

Beginning	Middle	End
Who is your character?	**What happens to them?**	**How do they change?**
-------------------------	-------------------------	-------------------------
-------------------------	-------------------------	-------------------------

good things

What shape does your story take? Draw it here and label the parts.

beginning   middle   end

bad things

MY
STORY

Write your story here!

MY
STORY

MY WRITING CHECKLIST

STORY AND STRUCTURE (6/22 MARKS)

My story:

- ◯ Introduces the character – what they look like, how they feel
- ◯ Describes the setting – what the character can see and hear
- ◯ Gets the reader's attention with a clever opening
- ◯ Has a character that changes – they overcome challenges or problems
- ◯ Has a clear beginning, middle, and end
- ◯ Makes sense and sticks to the topic

LANGUAGE (6/22 MARKS)

I have used:

- ◯ **Show, not tell** (e.g. facial expressions, body language, actions, dialogue)
- ◯ Lots of colourful vocabulary that draws the reader in
- ◯ Descriptive adjectives that help the reader imagine the character and setting
- ◯ Strong verbs that show what the characters are doing
- ◯ Dialogue to bring them to life
- ◯ All past tense or all present tense throughout the story

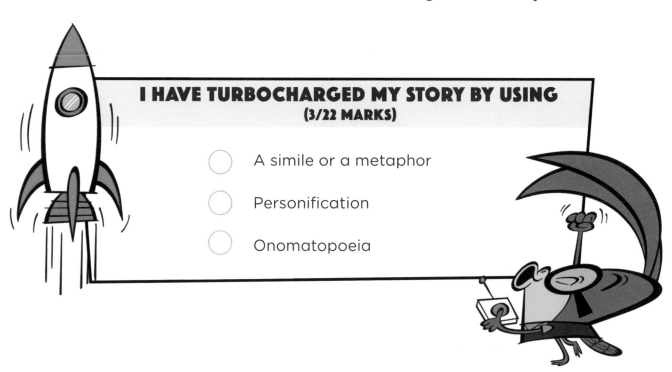

I HAVE TURBOCHARGED MY STORY BY USING
(3/22 MARKS)

- ◯ A simile or a metaphor
- ◯ Personification
- ◯ Onomatopoeia

MY WRITING CHECKLIST

SPELLING AND PUNCTUATION
(5/22 MARKS)

I have used correct punctuation and a range of sentence length to vary the pace:

- ◯ Capital letters and full stops
- ◯ Correct spelling
- ◯ Question marks at the end of questions
- ◯ Complex sentences
- ◯ At least one short, punchy sentence

PRESENTATION
(2/22 MARKS)

My story is easy to read because it uses:

- ◯ Neat handwriting
- ◯ Paragraphs for each idea or part of the story

FINAL SCORE

/ 22

STORY KIT 10

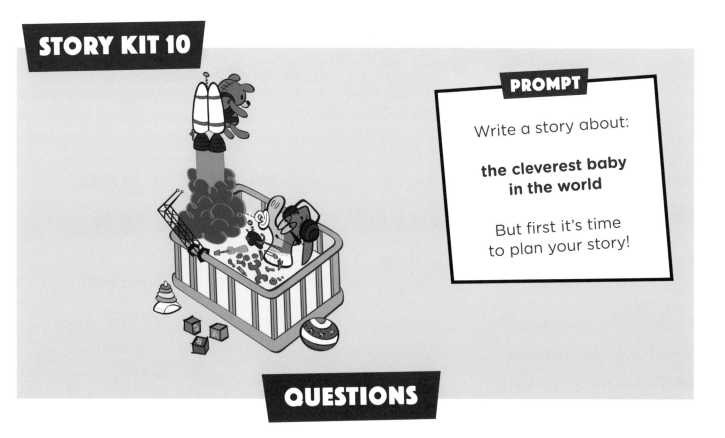

PROMPT

Write a story about:

**the cleverest baby
in the world**

But first it's time
to plan your story!

QUESTIONS

Who is your character?

1. What kind of personality does your character have? Are they friendly or mean?

2. What do they look like? What are they wearing?

3. Where does your character live? Do they live with family or alone?

4. Do they have lots of friends?

5. What motivates your character?

What happens to them?

1. How did this baby become the cleverest baby in the world?

2. What do they know lots about? History? Art? Music? Science?

3. What do they not know lots about?

4. How do people respond to the cleverest baby in the world? Do they respect them or fear them?

5. What responsibilities come with being the cleverest baby in the world?

How do they change?

1. What have they learned about themselves?

2. What lesson have they learned?

3. Do they keep their title of the world's cleverest baby?

4. Does your character have any regrets?

5. What would your character do differently next time?

VOCABULARY

Find the right words
Choose some word pairs, adjectives,
and verbs to use in your story.

WORD PAIRS

For example: colourful crib or logical brain

mastermind
evil
mysterious
secret
technological
•

prodigy
young
brilliant
creative
musical
•

baby
tiny
sleepy
beaming
mischievous
•

brain
logical
imaginative
rational
foggy
•

crib
colourful
wooden
narrow
cosy

toys
enormous
favourite
fluffy
mechanical

rocket
noisy
expensive
experimental
unstoppable

ADJECTIVES

genius
highbrow
expert
unexpected
mind-blowing
astonishing
unprecedented
unnerving
casual
nonchalant
record-breaking

VERBS

design
invent
program
build
crawl
suck
gnaw
wail
blubber
sob
sniffle
snuggle

STORY
GRAPH

Answer these questions and plot them on the graph of good things and bad things.

Beginning	Middle	End
Who is your character?	**What happens to them?**	**How do they change?**
-------------------------------	-------------------------------	-------------------------------
-------------------------------	-------------------------------	-------------------------------

good things

What shape does your story take? Draw it here and label the parts.

beginning   middle   end

bad things

MY
STORY

Write your story here!

MY WRITING CHECKLIST

STORY AND STRUCTURE (6/22 MARKS)

My story:

- ◯ Introduces the character – what they look like, how they feel

- ◯ Describes the setting – what the character can see and hear

- ◯ Gets the reader's attention with a clever opening

- ◯ Has a character that changes – they overcome challenges or problems

- ◯ Has a clear beginning, middle, and end

- ◯ Makes sense and sticks to the topic

LANGUAGE (6/22 MARKS)

I have used:

- ◯ **Show, not tell** (e.g. facial expressions, body language, actions, dialogue)

- ◯ Lots of colourful vocabulary that draws the reader in

- ◯ Descriptive adjectives that help the reader imagine the character and setting

- ◯ Strong verbs that show what the characters are doing

- ◯ Dialogue to bring them to life

- ◯ All past tense or all present tense throughout the story

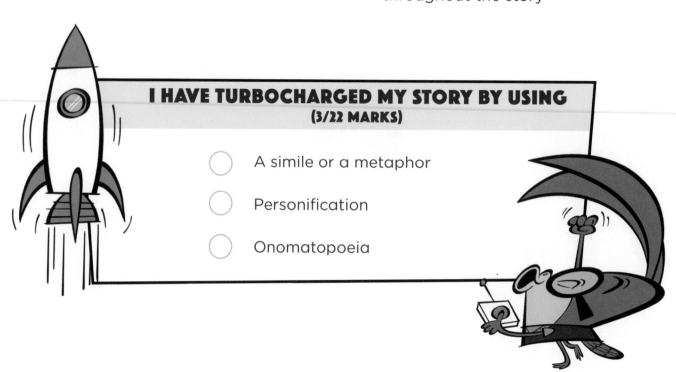

I HAVE TURBOCHARGED MY STORY BY USING
(3/22 MARKS)

- ◯ A simile or a metaphor

- ◯ Personification

- ◯ Onomatopoeia

SPELLING AND PUNCTUATION
(5/22 MARKS)

I have used correct punctuation and a range of sentence length to vary the pace:

○ Capital letters and full stops

○ Correct spelling

○ Question marks at the end of questions

○ Complex sentences

○ At least one short, punchy sentence

PRESENTATION
(2/22 MARKS)

My story is easy to read because it uses:

○ Neat handwriting

○ Paragraphs for each idea or part of the story

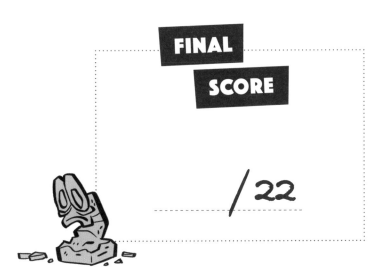

FINAL

SCORE

/ 22

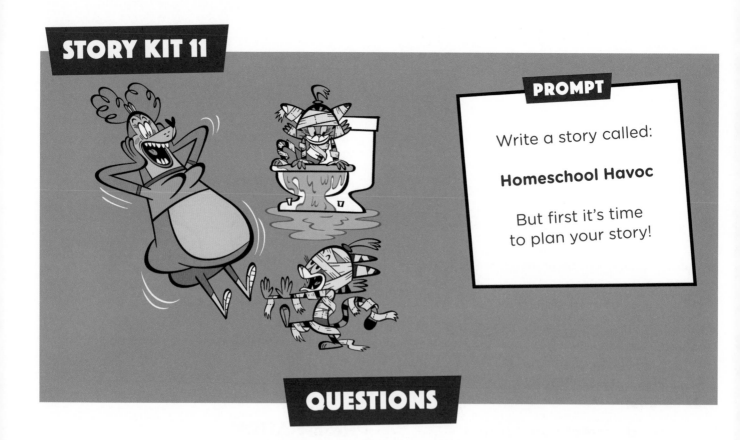

STORY KIT 11

PROMPT

Write a story called:

Homeschool Havoc

But first it's time to plan your story!

QUESTIONS

Who are your characters?

1. Who are the characters causing chaos?

2. What do all these characters look like?

3. What are their personalities like? Are they mischievous or well-behaved?

4. Is one of them older than the other? Do they get along well with each other?

5. Who is the other character? What is their personality like? Are they lenient or strict?

What happens to them?

1. What are they doing? Are they being playful or disruptive?

2. What have they covered themselves with? Do they look silly or sensible? How did they make these outfits?

3. Is anybody in charge? Have they lost control?

4. How does the person in charge feel about all of this? Are they pleased or angry?

5. Does something terrible happen? An accident? A crash? How is everything brought under control?

How do they change?

1. What do your characters learn from this?

2. Do they regret their actions?

3. Will they cause chaos again the next day?

4. Will the character in charge change their homeschooling approach?

5. What would everyone do differently next time?

VOCABULARY

WORD PAIRS

For example: muddy mess or gleeful havoc

cacophony	**toilet paper**	**prank**
joyful	missing	playful
growing	scrunched-up	harmless
constant	unravelled	mischievous
deafening	waterlogged	elaborate
•	•	•
havoc	**mirror**	**mess**
total	cracked	soggy
gleeful	foggy	muddy
widespread	shattered	tangled
unimaginable	graffitied	unsightly
•	•	
toilet	**water**	
clean	flowing	
clogged	rising	
leaky	gushing	
overflowing	murky	

ADJECTIVES

chaotic

wild

ferocious

disorderly

unruly

uncontrollable

hysterical

defiant

obstreperous

hyper

raucous

riotous

VERBS

unroll

cover

spray

splash

smash

shatter

trail

muck about

mess around

kick

punch

spin

twirl

skip

cartwheel

jump

leap

lunge

cackle

giggle

bounce

rebel

STORY GRAPH

Answer these questions and plot them on the graph of good things and bad things.

Beginning	Middle	End
Who is your character?	**What happens to them?**	**How do they change?**

good things

What shape does your story take? Draw it here and label the parts.

beginning   middle   end

bad things

MY
STORY

Write your story here!

MY STORY

MY WRITING CHECKLIST

STORY AND STRUCTURE (6/22 MARKS)

My story:

○ Introduces the character – what they look like, how they feel

○ Describes the setting – what the character can see and hear

○ Gets the reader's attention with a clever opening

○ Has a character that changes – they overcome challenges or problems

○ Has a clear beginning, middle, and end

○ Makes sense and sticks to the topic

LANGUAGE (6/22 MARKS)

I have used:

○ **Show, not tell** (e.g. facial expressions, body language, actions, dialogue)

○ Lots of colourful vocabulary that draws the reader in

○ Descriptive adjectives that help the reader imagine the character and setting

○ Strong verbs that show what the characters are doing

○ Dialogue to bring them to life

○ All past tense or all present tense throughout the story

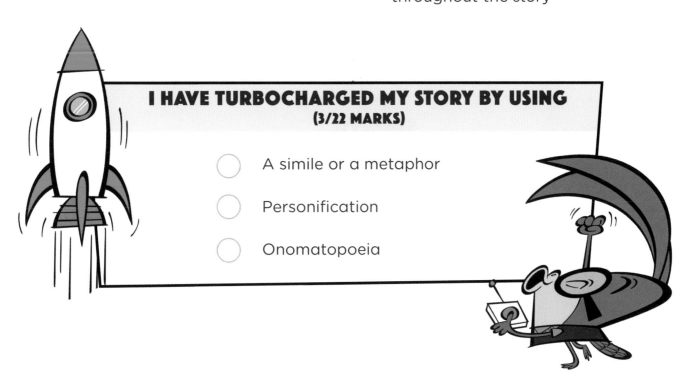

I HAVE TURBOCHARGED MY STORY BY USING
(3/22 MARKS)

○ A simile or a metaphor

○ Personification

○ Onomatopoeia

MY WRITING CHECKLIST

SPELLING AND PUNCTUATION
(5/22 MARKS)

I have used correct punctuation and a range of sentence length to vary the pace:

◯ Capital letters and full stops

◯ Correct spelling

◯ Question marks at the end of questions

◯ Complex sentences

◯ At least one short, punchy sentence

PRESENTATION
(2/22 MARKS)

My story is easy to read because it uses:

◯ Neat handwriting

◯ Paragraphs for each idea or part of the story

FINAL SCORE

_____ / 22

STORY KIT 12

PROMPT

Write a story called:

The Burger Bandit is Back

But first it's time to plan your story!

QUESTIONS

Who is your character?

1. How long has the detective been searching for the Burger Bandit?

2. Who is this detective? What does the detective want?

3. Who is the Burger Bandit? What do they do? Why do they do it?

4. What do they look like?

5. Is their identity a secret?

What happens to them?

1. Where does the Burger Bandit strike this time? Is it a new part of town or the same place as before?

2. What do these burgers look, smell, and taste like?

3. How does everyone else feel about the Burger Bandit? Do they respect and admire the bandit? Do they hate and fear the bandit?

4. How does everyone in the town feel about the detective?

5. Does the detective catch the bandit? If so how? With a clever trap? Or do they catch the bandit by accident?

How do they change?

1. What will the detective do now?

2. Is the detective proud of their work?

3. Has the bandit learned a lesson or will they plot to steal again?

4. What would the detective do differently next time?

5. What case will the detective take on next?

VOCABULARY

Find the right words
Choose some word pairs, adjectives,
and verbs to use in your story.

WORD PAIRS

For example: botched heist or skilled thief

heist	**thief**	**detective**
daring	skilled	famous
brazen	petty	undercover
botched	sneaky	bumbling
notorious	unidentified	disguised
•	•	•

burger	**victims**	**clue**
juicy	unlucky	first
greasy	innocent	important
vegan	unsuspecting	hidden
succulent	defenceless	baffling
		tell-tale

ADJECTIVES

clandestine

stealthy

wanted

prolific

greedy

unstoppable

VERBS

steal

grab

sneak

creep

gorge

track

decipher

discover

unearth

solve

ambush

surprise

GRAPH

Answer these questions and plot them on the graph of good things and bad things.

Beginning	Middle	End
Who is your character?	**What happens to them?**	**How do they change?**
------------------------------	------------------------------	------------------------------
------------------------------	------------------------------	------------------------------

good things

What shape does your story take? Draw it here and label the parts.

O - ●

beginning   **middle**   **end**

bad things

MY STORY

Write your story here!

MY WRITING CHECKLIST

STORY AND STRUCTURE (6/22 MARKS)

My story:

○ Introduces the character – what they look like, how they feel

○ Describes the setting – what the character can see and hear

○ Gets the reader's attention with a clever opening

○ Has a character that changes – they overcome challenges or problems

○ Has a clear beginning, middle, and end

○ Makes sense and sticks to the topic

LANGUAGE (6/22 MARKS)

I have used:

○ **Show, not tell** (e.g. facial expressions, body language, actions, dialogue)

○ Lots of colourful vocabulary that draws the reader in

○ Descriptive adjectives that help the reader imagine the character and setting

○ Strong verbs that show what the characters are doing

○ Dialogue to bring them to life

○ All past tense or all present tense throughout the story

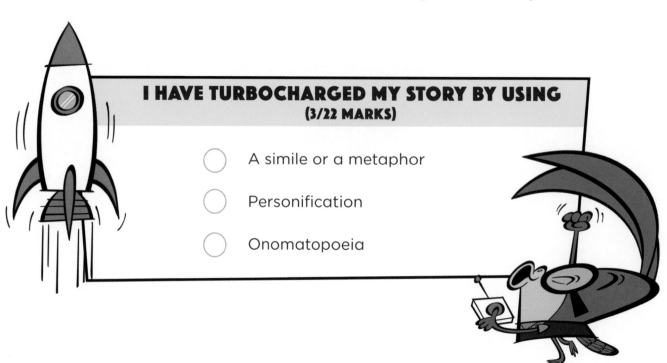

I HAVE TURBOCHARGED MY STORY BY USING
(3/22 MARKS)

○ A simile or a metaphor

○ Personification

○ Onomatopoeia

SPELLING AND PUNCTUATION
(5/22 MARKS)

I have used correct punctuation and a range of sentence length to vary the pace:

○ Capital letters and full stops

○ Correct spelling

○ Question marks at the end of questions

○ Complex sentences

○ At least one short, punchy sentence

PRESENTATION
(2/22 MARKS)

My story is easy to read because it uses:

○ Neat handwriting

○ Paragraphs for each idea or part of the story

FINAL

SCORE

_____ / 22

STORY KIT 13

PROMPT

Write a story about:

a kid who discovers they can talk to animals

But first it's time to plan your story!

QUESTIONS

Who is your character?

1. What type of personality does your character have? Are they kind or mean?

2. What do they look like? What are they wearing?

3. What motivates your character?

4. How do they feel about animals?

5. Do they have lots of pets?

What happens to them?

1. How do they discover that they can talk to animals?

2. Which animals can they talk to? Which animal do they get along best with? Which do they get along worst with?

3. What secrets does your character uncover talking to the animals?

4. What will your character do with this amazing skill?

5. Can anyone else in the world talk to animals?

How do they change?

1. How has your character's life changed now that they can talk to animals?

2. What has your character learned?

3. Is there anything about talking to animals that is not good?

4. How do your character's friends feel about the changes?

5. Will your character tell anybody else about this amazing skill? Why or why not?

VOCABULARY

Find the right words
Choose some word pairs, adjectives,
and verbs to use in your story.

WORD PAIRS

For example: shy kid or delicate butterfly

kid

shy

unusual

special

gifted

•

snake

deadly

venomous

harmless

slithering

•

ladybird

shiny

gorgeous

petite

elegant

•

squirrel

bushy-tailed

scampering

frightened

nimble

jungle

lush

dense

deep

impenetrable

•

parrot

flightless

talkative

squawking

endangered

•

lizard

flying

scaly

bearded

two-headed

secret

guarded

shocking

well-kept

profound

•

owl

sooty

mottled

solemn

nocturnal

•

butterfly

delicate

tropical

fluttering

endangered

ADJECTIVES

friendly

rowdy

witty

sly

prickly

loping

supportive

grouchy

cacophonous

unexpected

secluded

bubbly

energetic

fluttering

slow-moving

sluggish

welcoming

excitable

agreeable

polite

courteous

unfriendly

suspicious

disagreeable

VERBS

speak

communicate

discuss

joke

play

giggle

meet

gather

call

sing

tweet

hiss

whisper

growl

buzz

reveal

discover

explain

understand

empathise

sympathise

STORY

GRAPH

Answer these questions and plot them on the graph of good things and bad things.

Beginning	Middle	End
Who is your character?	**What happens to them?**	**How do they change?**
-------------------------------	-------------------------------	-------------------------------
-------------------------------	-------------------------------	-------------------------------

good things

What shape does your story take? Draw it here and label the parts.

beginning   middle   end

bad things

MY STORY

Write your story here!

MY STORY

MY WRITING CHECKLIST

STORY AND STRUCTURE (6/22 MARKS)

My story:

- ◯ Introduces the character – what they look like, how they feel

- ◯ Describes the setting – what the character can see and hear

- ◯ Gets the reader's attention with a clever opening

- ◯ Has a character that changes – they overcome challenges or problems

- ◯ Has a clear beginning, middle, and end

- ◯ Makes sense and sticks to the topic

LANGUAGE (6/22 MARKS)

I have used:

- ◯ **Show, not tell** (e.g. facial expressions, body language, actions, dialogue)

- ◯ Lots of colourful vocabulary that draws the reader in

- ◯ Descriptive adjectives that help the reader imagine the character and setting

- ◯ Strong verbs that show what the characters are doing

- ◯ Dialogue to bring them to life

- ◯ All past tense or all present tense throughout the story

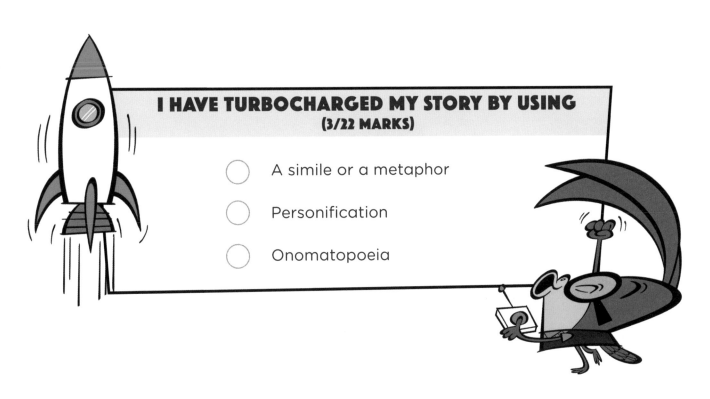

I HAVE TURBOCHARGED MY STORY BY USING
(3/22 MARKS)

- ◯ A simile or a metaphor

- ◯ Personification

- ◯ Onomatopoeia

MY WRITING CHECKLIST

SPELLING AND PUNCTUATION
(5/22 MARKS)

I have used correct punctuation and a range of sentence length to vary the pace:

- ( ) Capital letters and full stops

- ( ) Correct spelling

- ( ) Question marks at the end of questions

- ( ) Complex sentences

- ( ) At least one short, punchy sentence

PRESENTATION
(2/22 MARKS)

My story is easy to read because it uses:

- ( ) Neat handwriting

- ( ) Paragraphs for each idea or part of the story

FINAL SCORE

____ / 22

PROMPT

Write a story called:

The Man Who Lived In A Tree

But first it's time to plan your story!

QUESTIONS

Who is your character?

1. What type of personality does your character have?

2. Do they love or hate nature?

3. How long has your character lived in a tree?

4. What made them decide to move into a tree?

5. What are their biggest fears?

What happens to them?

1. How did they find the right tree to live in?

2. How much stuff do they have with them?

3. What is the most difficult part of living in a tree?

4. What do they like best about it?

5. What do their friends think of their unusual home?

How do they change?

1. Will your character live in the tree forever?

2. Will they move back into a house?

3. If they could change one thing about this tree what would it be?

4. What have they learned from living in this tree?

5. How has living in the tree changed their outlook?

VOCABULARY

WORD PAIRS

For example: eerie echo or honest answer

echo
hollow
booming
eerie
resounding
•

answer
honest
vague
emphatic
incoherent
•

bed
foldable
uncomfortable
snug
makeshift
•

interview
exclusive
candid
revealing
scandalous
•

lifestyle
simple
sustainable
outdoor
hectic
•

moss
thick
damp
spongy
velvety
•

question
obvious
difficult
leading
probing

home
temporary
poky
spacious
cramped

bark
smooth
rough
crumbling
gnarled

ADJECTIVES

damp
muddy
distant
quiet
muffled
hollow
reverberating
unfriendly
hesitant
solitary
welcoming
excitable
eloquent
raging
content
serene
gracious
courteous
respectful
admirable
upright
vertical
horizontal
splintered

VERBS

shout
yell
mumble
ask
inquire
profess
confess
divulge
admit
explain

STORY

GRAPH

Answer these questions and plot them on the graph of good things and bad things.

Beginning	Middle	End
Who is your character?	**What happens to them?**	**How do they change?**
-------------------	-------------------	-------------------
-------------------	-------------------	-------------------

good things

What shape does your story take? Draw it here and label the parts.

beginning　　　　　**middle**　　　　　**end**

bad things

MY STORY

Write your story here!

MY WRITING CHECKLIST

STORY AND STRUCTURE (6/22 MARKS)

My story:

- ◯ Introduces the character - what they look like, how they feel

- ◯ Describes the setting - what the character can see and hear

- ◯ Gets the reader's attention with a clever opening

- ◯ Has a character that changes - they overcome challenges or problems

- ◯ Has a clear beginning, middle, and end

- ◯ Makes sense and sticks to the topic

LANGUAGE (6/22 MARKS)

I have used:

- ◯ **Show, not tell** (e.g. facial expressions, body language, actions, dialogue)

- ◯ Lots of colourful vocabulary that draws the reader in

- ◯ Descriptive adjectives that help the reader imagine the character and setting

- ◯ Strong verbs that show what the characters are doing

- ◯ Dialogue to bring them to life

- ◯ All past tense or all present tense throughout the story

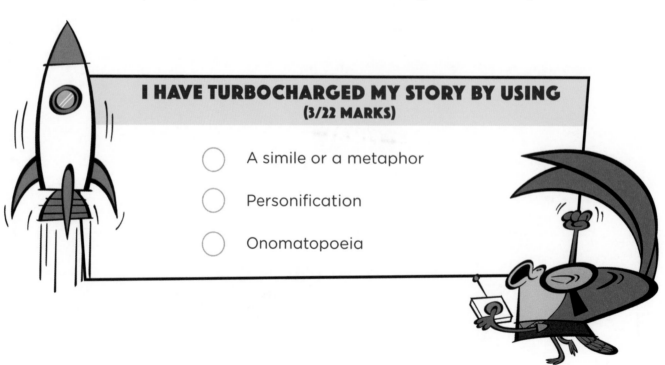

I HAVE TURBOCHARGED MY STORY BY USING
(3/22 MARKS)

- ◯ A simile or a metaphor

- ◯ Personification

- ◯ Onomatopoeia

SPELLING AND PUNCTUATION
(5/22 MARKS)

I have used correct punctuation and a range of sentence length to vary the pace:

○ Capital letters and full stops

○ Correct spelling

○ Question marks at the end of questions

○ Complex sentences

○ At least one short, punchy sentence

PRESENTATION
(2/22 MARKS)

My story is easy to read because it uses:

○ Neat handwriting

○ Paragraphs for each idea or part of the story

FINAL

SCORE

____ / 22

QUESTIONS

Who is your character?

1. What type of personality does your character have? Are they proactive or lazy?

2. What do they look like? What are they wearing?

3. What motivates your character?

4. How do they feel about doing their homework?

5. What do they like to do instead of homework? Play football? Bake? Code?

What happens to them?

1. What was the homework they had been set?

2. Who was the teacher who set it?

3. Why didn't they do their homework?

4. What excuse did they give to the teacher? Why was it so ridiculous?

5. Did the teacher believe the excuse? If not, what punishment does the character receive?

How do they change?

1. What lesson has the character learned?

2. What would they do differently next time?

3. Will they always do their homework from now on?

4. Will they keep making up ridiculous excuses?

5. How has this experience changed their outlook?

VOCABULARY

WORD PAIRS

For example: greedy goblin or reasonable excuse

excuse	**lie**	**homework**
reasonable	brazen	online
flimsy	outrageous	missing
concocted	believable	impossible
implausible	audacious	half-finished
•	•	•
tornado	**dragon**	**flames**
sudden	fierce	blazing
whirling	monstrous	flickering
devastating	fire-breathing	devouring
disastrous	gargantuan	crackling
•	•	•
alien	**goblin**	**unicorn**
green	greedy	talking
one-eyed	lonely	magical
humanoid	mischievous	winged
telepathic	villainous	elusive

ADJECTIVES

apologetic
confused
rambling
jumbled
muddled
obscure
implausible
preposterous
ridiculous
absurd
incredible
unbelievable
nonsensical

VERBS

lie
fib
invent
imagine
tremble
hesitate
freeze
sweat
perspire
ramble
destroy
vanish
burn
swallow

STORY
GRAPH

Answer these questions and plot them on the graph of good things and bad things.

Beginning	Middle	End
Who is your character?	**What happens to them?**	**How do they change?**
-------------------------------	-------------------------------	-------------------------------
-------------------------------	-------------------------------	-------------------------------

good things

What shape does your story take? Draw it here and label the parts.

beginning   middle   end

bad things

MY
STORY

Write your story here!

MY STORY

MY WRITING CHECKLIST

STORY AND STRUCTURE (6/22 MARKS)

My story:

- ◯ Introduces the character – what they look like, how they feel
- ◯ Describes the setting – what the character can see and hear
- ◯ Gets the reader's attention with a clever opening
- ◯ Has a character that changes – they overcome challenges or problems
- ◯ Has a clear beginning, middle, and end
- ◯ Makes sense and sticks to the topic

LANGUAGE (6/22 MARKS)

I have used:

- ◯ **Show, not tell** (e.g. facial expressions, body language, actions, dialogue)
- ◯ Lots of colourful vocabulary that draws the reader in
- ◯ Descriptive adjectives that help the reader imagine the character and setting
- ◯ Strong verbs that show what the characters are doing
- ◯ Dialogue to bring them to life
- ◯ All past tense or all present tense throughout the story

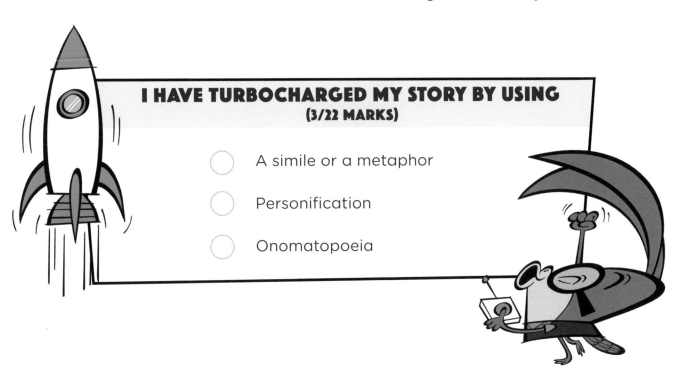

I HAVE TURBOCHARGED MY STORY BY USING
(3/22 MARKS)

- ◯ A simile or a metaphor
- ◯ Personification
- ◯ Onomatopoeia

MY WRITING CHECKLIST

SPELLING AND PUNCTUATION
(5/22 MARKS)

I have used correct punctuation and a range of sentence length to vary the pace:

◯ Capital letters and full stops

◯ Correct spelling

◯ Question marks at the end of questions

◯ Complex sentences

◯ At least one short, punchy sentence

PRESENTATION
(2/22 MARKS)

My story is easy to read because it uses:

◯ Neat handwriting

◯ Paragraphs for each idea or part of the story

FINAL SCORE

_____ / 22

STORY KIT 16

PROMPT

Write a story called:

Don't Litter... Recycle!

But first it's time to plan your story!

QUESTIONS

Who is your character?

1. What type of personality does your character have?

2. What do they look like? What are they wearing?

3. Do they feel strongly about recycling or do they not care?

4. What motivates them?

5. What is their biggest fear?

What happens to them?

1. Where are they when they see someone littering?

2. How do they feel when they see the littering?

3. How do they react? Do they say something? Or stay silent?

4. What do they say to the litterer?

5. Will they befriend the litterer? Or tell them off?

How do they change?

1. What has the character learned from this experience?

2. Do they wish they had responded differently?

3. How will they react next time?

4. Has this experience changed their outlook?

5. Has this experience inspired them to try something new?

VOCABULARY

WORD PAIRS

For example: cheap plastic or healthy oceans

plastic	**deforestation**	**wildlife**
cheap	rapid	rich
single-use	reduced	abundant
harmful	excessive	diverse
discarded	rampant	endangered
•	•	•
particles	**oceans**	**landfill**
plastic	filthy	overflowing
microscopic	polluted	vast
toxic	healthy	toxic
airborne	teeming	hazardous

ADJECTIVES

organised

responsible

dutiful

collaborative

shared

future-proof

sustainable

harmful

destructive

diverse

habitable

dangerous

pointless

shameful

shocking

simple

straightforward

VERBS

save

conserve

protect

pollute

destroy

use up waste

STORY
GRAPH

Answer these questions and plot them on the graph of good things and bad things.

Beginning	Middle	End
Who is your character?	**What happens to them?**	**How do they change?**
-------------------------	-------------------------	-------------------------
-------------------------	-------------------------	-------------------------

good things

What shape does your story take? Draw it here and label the parts.

beginning   middle   end

bad things

MY STORY

Write your story here!

MY WRITING CHECKLIST

STORY AND STRUCTURE (6/22 MARKS)

My story:

○ Introduces the character - what they look like, how they feel

○ Describes the setting - what the character can see and hear

○ Gets the reader's attention with a clever opening

○ Has a character that changes - they overcome challenges or problems

○ Has a clear beginning, middle, and end

○ Makes sense and sticks to the topic

LANGUAGE (6/22 MARKS)

I have used:

○ **Show, not tell** (e.g. facial expressions, body language, actions, dialogue)

○ Lots of colourful vocabulary that draws the reader in

○ Descriptive adjectives that help the reader imagine the character and setting

○ Strong verbs that show what the characters are doing

○ Dialogue to bring them to life

○ All past tense or all present tense throughout the story

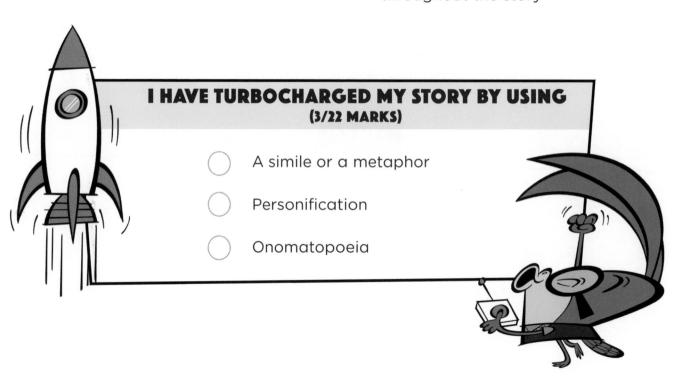

I HAVE TURBOCHARGED MY STORY BY USING
(3/22 MARKS)

○ A simile or a metaphor

○ Personification

○ Onomatopoeia

SPELLING AND PUNCTUATION
(5/22 MARKS)

I have used correct punctuation and a range of sentence length to vary the pace:

○ Capital letters and full stops

○ Correct spelling

○ Question marks at the end of questions

○ Complex sentences

○ At least one short, punchy sentence

PRESENTATION
(2/22 MARKS)

My story is easy to read because it uses:

○ Neat handwriting

○ Paragraphs for each idea or part of the story

FINAL

SCORE

_____ / 22

STORY KIT 17

PROMPT

Write a story about:

a fearless scientist who searches tirelessly for a cure for everything

But first it's time to plan your story!

QUESTIONS

Who is your character?

1. Who is this fearless scientist?

2. How long have they been a scientist?

3. What are their likes and dislikes?

4. What do they do to help themselves concentrate?

5. What kind of personality does it take to be a good scientist?

What happens to them?

1. How long have they been searching for the cure?

2. What inspired them to search for this magical cure?

3. What type of experiments are they doing to find the cure?

4. Are they close to finding the cure?

5. What is the greatest challenge when creating this cure?

How do they change?

1. What have they learned from their experience?

2. Did they make any mistakes along the way?

3. Is there anything they wish they had done differently?

4. How will they celebrate when they find the cure?

5. Have they already started to think about their next project? What will it be?

VOCABULARY

Find the right words

Find the right words

Choose some word pairs, adjectives, and verbs to use in your story.

WORD PAIRS

For example: ruined sample or modern lab

test tubes	**wires**	**lab**
clean	thin	modern
sterile	coated	medical
labelled	tangled	spotless
corked	insulated	high-tech
•	•	•

sample	**concoction**	**cure**
pure	deadly	natural
ruined	mysterious	effective
genetic	disgusting	mystery
radioactive	ingenious	miraculous
•	•	

idea	**side effects**
simple	common
genius	rare
radical	positive
ambitious	alarming

ADJECTIVES

medical

medicinal

effective

laborious

arduous

tedious

meticulous

strenuous

detailed

minuscule

precise

accurate

sloppy

mistaken

erroneous

anomalous

VERBS

mix

heat

stir

extract

measure

transfer

dissolve

evaporate

dilute

wash

drop

absorb

scoop

scratch

light

burn

shake

test

experiment

find

discover

attempt

repeat

STORY GRAPH

Answer these questions and plot them on the graph of good things and bad things.

Beginning	Middle	End
Who is your character?	**What happens to them?**	**How do they change?**

What shape does your story take? Draw it here and label the parts.

good things

beginning   **middle**   **end**

bad things

MY
STORY

Write your story here!

MY STORY

MY WRITING CHECKLIST

STORY AND STRUCTURE (6/22 MARKS)

My story:

- ○ Introduces the character – what they look like, how they feel
- ○ Describes the setting – what the character can see and hear
- ○ Gets the reader's attention with a clever opening
- ○ Has a character that changes – they overcome challenges or problems
- ○ Has a clear beginning, middle, and end
- ○ Makes sense and sticks to the topic

LANGUAGE (6/22 MARKS)

I have used:

- ○ **Show, not tell** (e.g. facial expressions, body language, actions, dialogue)
- ○ Lots of colourful vocabulary that draws the reader in
- ○ Descriptive adjectives that help the reader imagine the character and setting
- ○ Strong verbs that show what the characters are doing
- ○ Dialogue to bring them to life
- ○ All past tense or all present tense throughout the story

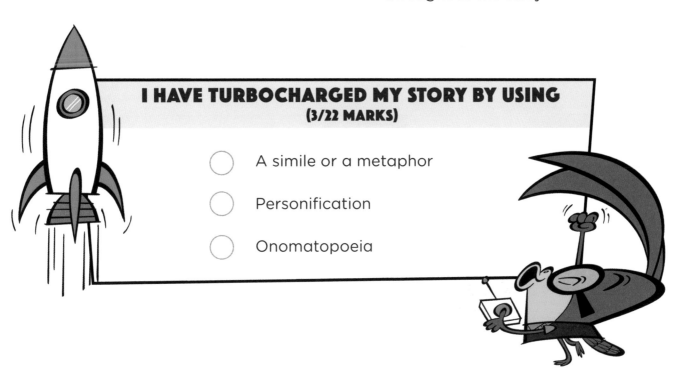

I HAVE TURBOCHARGED MY STORY BY USING
(3/22 MARKS)

- ○ A simile or a metaphor
- ○ Personification
- ○ Onomatopoeia

MY WRITING CHECKLIST

SPELLING AND PUNCTUATION
(5/22 MARKS)

I have used correct punctuation and a range of sentence length to vary the pace:

- ◯ Capital letters and full stops

- ◯ Correct spelling

- ◯ Question marks at the end of questions

- ◯ Complex sentences

- ◯ At least one short, punchy sentence

PRESENTATION
(2/22 MARKS)

My story is easy to read because it uses:

- ◯ Neat handwriting

- ◯ Paragraphs for each idea or part of the story

FINAL

SCORE

_____ / 22

PROMPT

Write a story called:

Running for President!

But first it's time to plan your story!

QUESTIONS

Who is your character?

1. What type of personality does your character have?

2. Why do they want to be president?

3. What do they want to be the president of? The class? The country? The whole wide world?

4. What are your character's best personality traits? How will they help them in their role as president?

5. What are their biggest weaknesses?

What happens to them?

1. What is their campaign slogan?

2. What do they promise to do if they become president?

3. What is the biggest challenge they face while running for president?

4. How do they feel on the day of the election? Are they nervous or excited?

5. What happens next? Do they win or lose?

How do they change?

1. What does your character learn from this experience?

2. Do they wish they had done anything differently?

3. Do they have any regrets?

4. What will they do if they are elected? How will they react?

5. What will they do if they are not elected? Will they try again next time or will they do something else?

VOCABULARY

WORD PAIRS

For example: major crisis or respected leader

leader	**experience**	**skills**
respected	hands-on	creative
inspiring	valuable	strategic
charismatic	relevant	impressive
visionary	rewarding	interpersonal
•	•	•
election	**crisis**	**charisma**
local	major	natural
historic	sudden	undeniable
presidential	looming	powerful
fraudulent	escalating	effortless
•	•	
issues	**solution**	
serious	simple	
pressing	lasting	
environmental	effective	
complex	temporary	

ADJECTIVES

inspirational
trustworthy
reliable
truthful
honest
candid
charismatic
likeable
genuine
meaningful
urgent
important
crucial
essential
peaceful
effective
efficient
pragmatic
problem-solving
responsible

VERBS

campaign
trust
empower
vote
elect
improve
implement
support
represent
negotiate
lead
understand
listen

STORY GRAPH

Answer these questions and plot them on the graph of good things and bad things.

Beginning	Middle	End
Who is your character?	**What happens to them?**	**How do they change?**

- -

- -

good things

What shape does your story take? Draw it here and label the parts.

beginning   middle   end

bad things

MY STORY

Write your story here!

MY WRITING CHECKLIST

STORY AND STRUCTURE (6/22 MARKS)

My story:

- ○ Introduces the character – what they look like, how they feel

- ○ Describes the setting – what the character can see and hear

- ○ Gets the reader's attention with a clever opening

- ○ Has a character that changes – they overcome challenges or problems

- ○ Has a clear beginning, middle, and end

- ○ Makes sense and sticks to the topic

LANGUAGE (6/22 MARKS)

I have used:

- ○ **Show, not tell** (e.g. facial expressions, body language, actions, dialogue)

- ○ Lots of colourful vocabulary that draws the reader in

- ○ Descriptive adjectives that help the reader imagine the character and setting

- ○ Strong verbs that show what the characters are doing

- ○ Dialogue to bring them to life

- ○ All past tense or all present tense throughout the story

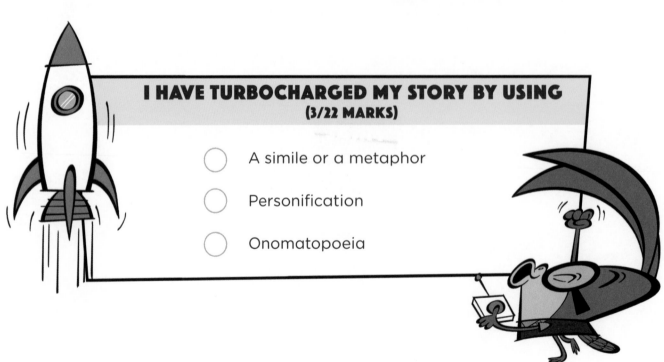

I HAVE TURBOCHARGED MY STORY BY USING (3/22 MARKS)

- ○ A simile or a metaphor

- ○ Personification

- ○ Onomatopoeia

SPELLING AND PUNCTUATION
(5/22 MARKS)

I have used correct punctuation and a range of sentence length to vary the pace:

- ( ) Capital letters and full stops

- ( ) Correct spelling

- ( ) Question marks at the end of questions

- ( ) Complex sentences

- ( ) At least one short, punchy sentence

PRESENTATION
(2/22 MARKS)

My story is easy to read because it uses:

- ( ) Neat handwriting

- ( ) Paragraphs for each idea or part of the story

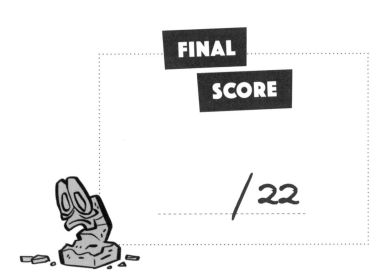

FINAL SCORE

_____ / 22

STORY KIT 19

PROMPT

Write a story called:

The Mix Up

But first it's time to plan your story!

QUESTIONS

Who is your character?

1. What type of personality does your character have?

2. What do they look like? Are they large or small?

3. What made them decide to go on holiday?

4. What type of holiday do they enjoy? Relaxing or adventurous?

5. What is their greatest fear about this holiday?

What happens to them?

1. How long is the journey? Do they have lots to carry?

2. Do they find their accommodation easily? How do they get there?

3. What does the accommodation look like from the outside? Do they try to go inside?

4. How do they feel when they see their accommodation?

5. What do they decide to do? Do they turn around and go home or do they stay?

How do they change?

1. How does your character deal with the situation?

2. What has the character learned about themselves?

3. Would they do anything differently next time?

4. Where will they go on their next trip?

5. Will they be more thorough when they book their accommodation from now on?

VOCABULARY

WORD PAIRS

For example: broken GPS or honest review

accommodation	**journey**	**review**
basic	neverending	honest
uninviting	unforgettable	glowing
poky	arduous	lukewarm
quaint	treacherous	scathing
•	•	•

luggage	**GPS**	**hut**
bulky	accurate	lonely
overstuffed	broken	thatched
damaged	reliable	ramshackle
abandoned	malfunctioning	dilapidated

ADJECTIVES	**VERBS**
exhausted	trek
bemused	lug
baffled	hike
disappointed	traverse
underwhelmed	arrive
flabbergasted	glimpse
shocked	spot
appalled	take in
disgusted	examine
speechless	wonder

STORY

GRAPH

Answer these questions and plot them on the graph of good things and bad things.

Beginning	Middle	End
Who is your character?	**What happens to them?**	**How do they change?**
-------------------------------	-------------------------------	-------------------------------
-------------------------------	-------------------------------	-------------------------------

good things

What shape does your story take? Draw it here and label the parts.

beginning   middle   end

bad things

MY STORY

Write your story here!

MY
STORY

MY WRITING CHECKLIST

STORY AND STRUCTURE (6/22 MARKS)

My story:

- ◯ Introduces the character – what they look like, how they feel
- ◯ Describes the setting – what the character can see and hear
- ◯ Gets the reader's attention with a clever opening
- ◯ Has a character that changes – they overcome challenges or problems
- ◯ Has a clear beginning, middle, and end
- ◯ Makes sense and sticks to the topic

LANGUAGE (6/22 MARKS)

I have used:

- ◯ **Show, not tell** (e.g. facial expressions, body language, actions, dialogue)
- ◯ Lots of colourful vocabulary that draws the reader in
- ◯ Descriptive adjectives that help the reader imagine the character and setting
- ◯ Strong verbs that show what the characters are doing
- ◯ Dialogue to bring them to life
- ◯ All past tense or all present tense throughout the story

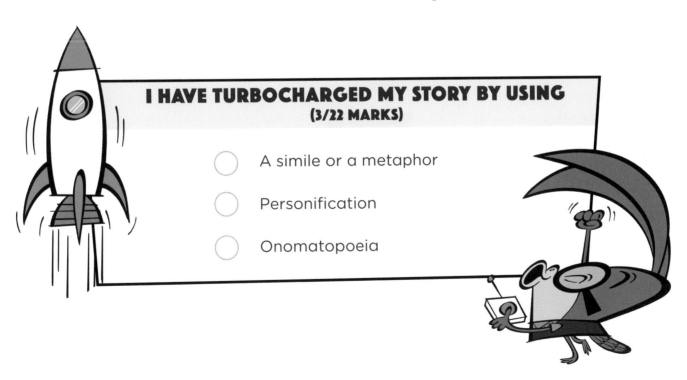

I HAVE TURBOCHARGED MY STORY BY USING
(3/22 MARKS)

- ◯ A simile or a metaphor
- ◯ Personification
- ◯ Onomatopoeia

MY WRITING CHECKLIST

SPELLING AND PUNCTUATION
(5/22 MARKS)

I have used correct punctuation and a range of sentence length to vary the pace:

○ Capital letters and full stops

○ Correct spelling

○ Question marks at the end of questions

○ Complex sentences

○ At least one short, punchy sentence

PRESENTATION
(2/22 MARKS)

My story is easy to read because it uses:

○ Neat handwriting

○ Paragraphs for each idea or part of the story

FINAL SCORE

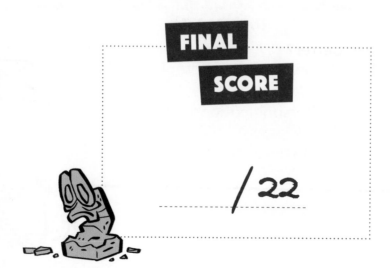

/ 22

STORY KIT 20

PROMPT

Write a story about:

someone trying to clean up the world before it's too late

But first it's time to plan your story!

QUESTIONS

Who is your character?

1. What type of personality does your character have?

2. What do they look like? What are they wearing?

3. Do they care about the environment?

4. What motivates your character?

5. What is their greatest fear?

What happens to them?

1. Why is your character trying to clean up the world?

2. What are the most incredible things about the world?

3. How can the planet be saved and nature be protected? What examples might your character give that everyone could do better? Drive less often? Use less plastic? Recycle?

4. Why is it important to your character that everyone makes these changes?

5. What will happen if nothing is done?

How do they change?

1. What does your character learn from this experience?

2. Do they wish they had responded differently?

3. Will they continue to try to clean up the world?

4. Will they give up trying to clean up the world?

5. Has this experience changed their outlook?

VOCABULARY

Find the right words
Choose some word pairs, adjectives,
and verbs to use in your story.

WORD PAIRS

For example: black fumes or efficient car

smog	**pollution**	**wasteland**
heavy	air	harsh
deadly	environmental	bleak
persistent	atmospheric	barren
impenetrable	marine	desolate
•	•	•

fumes	**car**	**sky**
black	electric	blue
thick	gas-guzzling	clear
hazardous	hybrid	hazy
acrid	efficient	dark
•	•	•

trees	**wind turbine**	**solar panels**
bushy	distant	broken
lush	spinning	efficient
young	towering	sustainable
newly planted	majestic	inconspicuous

ADJECTIVES

flooded
parched
polluted
dark
thick
dense
harmful
toxic
filthy
grimy
solar
green
environmental
eco-friendly
damaged

VERBS

guzzle
waste
litter
drive
recycle
reuse
cycle
decompose
plant
nurture
grow
filter
clean
spoil
repair
restore
rewild
exercise
replenish

STORY GRAPH

Answer these questions and plot them on the graph of good things and bad things.

Beginning	Middle	End
Who is your character?	**What happens to them?**	**How do they change?**
- - - - - - - - - - - - - - - -	- - - - - - - - - - - - - - - -	- - - - - - - - - - - - - - - -
- - - - - - - - - - - - - - - -	- - - - - - - - - - - - - - - -	- - - - - - - - - - - - - - - -

good things

What shape does your story take? Draw it here and label the parts.

O- ●

beginning   **middle**   **end**

bad things

MY STORY

Write your story here!

MY WRITING CHECKLIST

STORY AND STRUCTURE (6/22 MARKS)

My story:

- ◯ Introduces the character – what they look like, how they feel
- ◯ Describes the setting – what the character can see and hear
- ◯ Gets the reader's attention with a clever opening
- ◯ Has a character that changes – they overcome challenges or problems
- ◯ Has a clear beginning, middle, and end
- ◯ Makes sense and sticks to the topic

LANGUAGE (6/22 MARKS)

I have used:

- ◯ **Show, not tell** (e.g. facial expressions, body language, actions, dialogue)
- ◯ Lots of colourful vocabulary that draws the reader in
- ◯ Descriptive adjectives that help the reader imagine the character and setting
- ◯ Strong verbs that show what the characters are doing
- ◯ Dialogue to bring them to life
- ◯ All past tense or all present tense throughout the story

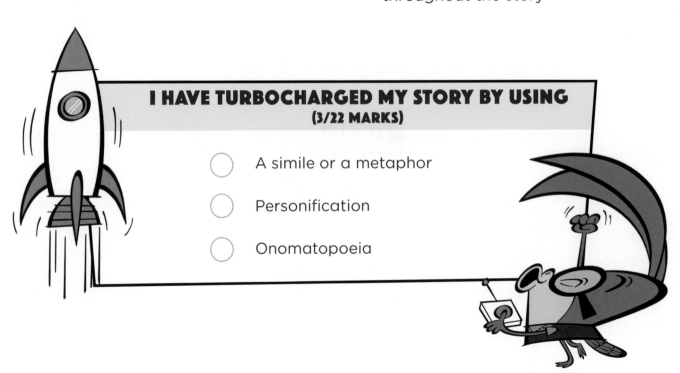

I HAVE TURBOCHARGED MY STORY BY USING
(3/22 MARKS)

- ◯ A simile or a metaphor
- ◯ Personification
- ◯ Onomatopoeia

SPELLING AND PUNCTUATION
(5/22 MARKS)

I have used correct punctuation and a range of sentence length to vary the pace:

◯ Capital letters and full stops

◯ Correct spelling

◯ Question marks at the end of questions

◯ Complex sentences

◯ At least one short, punchy sentence

PRESENTATION
(2/22 MARKS)

My story is easy to read because it uses:

◯ Neat handwriting

◯ Paragraphs for each idea or part of the story

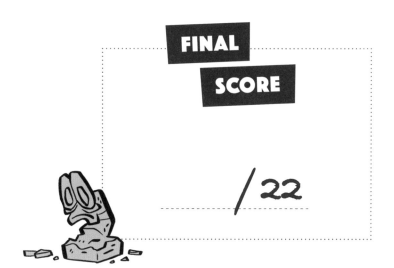

FINAL

SCORE

_____ / 22

STORY KIT 21

PROMPT

Write a story about:

a famous blogger who goes on an amazing holiday

But first it's time to plan your story!

QUESTIONS

Who is your character?

1. What type of personality does your character have?

2. What do they look like? What are they wearing?

3. How did they become a famous blogger?

4. What do they usually blog about? Are they a travel blogger or is this their first time abroad?

5. What motivated them to travel?

What happens to them?

1. Where have they gone on holiday?

2. What can they see, hear, smell, and taste on this holiday?

3. How do they feel about the holiday? Do they love it or hate it?

4. Does anything disastrous happen on their holiday? Or does it all go to plan?

5. What do they tell their followers about the holiday? Do they tell the truth? Or do they lie?

How do they change?

1. How does this trip change your character? Are they more relaxed or more stressed out?

2. Have they tried anything new? Have they learned anything about the local culture?

3. Would they recommend a trip like this to their followers?

4. What advice do they give their followers about the holiday?

5. Are they sad about going home or are they looking forward to it? Why?

VOCABULARY

Find the right words
Choose some word pairs, adjectives,
and verbs to use in your story.

WORD PAIRS

For example: crimson sunset or flip-flop sandals

sunset	**beach**	**sand**
fiery	sandy	golden
crimson	pristine	coarse
stunning	secluded	caked
breathtaking	picturesque	pristine
•	•	•
weather	**sun**	**smoothie**
warm	blazing	refreshing
balmy	scorching	organic
temperate	sinking	energising
sweltering	unforgiving	nutritious
•	•	•
sun hat	**sandals**	**sunglasses**
straw	flip-flop	vintage
wide-brimmed	strappy	over-sized
oversized	bejewelled	futuristic
distinctive	versatile	statement
•		

sunscreen

oily

waterproof

perfumed

tinted

ADJECTIVES

idyllic

balmy

dreamy

perfect

blissful

heavenly

rural

golden

fragrant

serene

tranquil

joyful

lighthearted

carefree

VERBS

fly

travel

lounge

chill

unwind

relax

refresh

kick back

paddle

amble

stroll

sunbathe

swim

splash

frolic

play

detox

STORY

GRAPH

Answer these questions and plot them on the graph of good things and bad things.

Beginning	Middle	End
Who is your character?	**What happens to them?**	**How do they change?**
----------------------------	----------------------------	----------------------------
----------------------------	----------------------------	----------------------------

good things

What shape does your story take? Draw it here and label the parts.

beginning   **middle**   **end**

bad things

MY STORY

Write your story here!

MY STORY

MY WRITING CHECKLIST

STORY AND STRUCTURE (6/22 MARKS)

My story:

◯ Introduces the character – what they look like, how they feel

◯ Describes the setting – what the character can see and hear

◯ Gets the reader's attention with a clever opening

◯ Has a character that changes – they overcome challenges or problems

◯ Has a clear beginning, middle, and end

◯ Makes sense and sticks to the topic

LANGUAGE (6/22 MARKS)

I have used:

◯ **Show, not tell** (e.g. facial expressions, body language, actions, dialogue)

◯ Lots of colourful vocabulary that draws the reader in

◯ Descriptive adjectives that help the reader imagine the character and setting

◯ Strong verbs that show what the characters are doing

◯ Dialogue to bring them to life

◯ All past tense or all present tense throughout the story

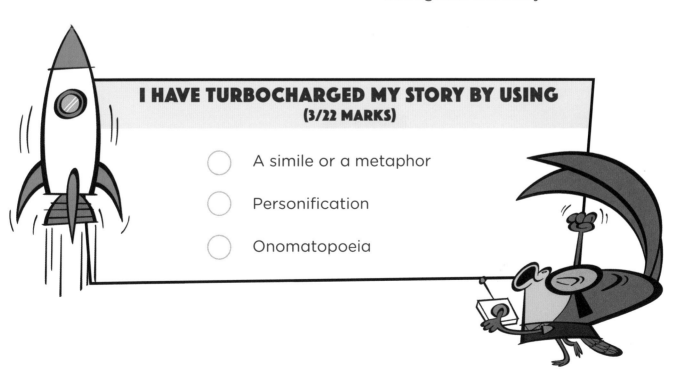

I HAVE TURBOCHARGED MY STORY BY USING
(3/22 MARKS)

◯ A simile or a metaphor

◯ Personification

◯ Onomatopoeia

MY WRITING CHECKLIST

SPELLING AND PUNCTUATION
(5/22 MARKS)

I have used correct punctuation and a range of sentence length to vary the pace:

- ◯ Capital letters and full stops
- ◯ Correct spelling
- ◯ Question marks at the end of questions
- ◯ Complex sentences
- ◯ At least one short, punchy sentence

PRESENTATION
(2/22 MARKS)

My story is easy to read because it uses:

- ◯ Neat handwriting
- ◯ Paragraphs for each idea or part of the story

FINAL SCORE

_____ / 22

ADDITIONAL INFORMATION:

National Curriculum Guidelines for Narrative Writing

Our mark schemes and checklists have been developed with teachers and assessment experts, and are in accordance with the national curriculum. For further reading, you can see highlights of the national curriculum below.

UK KS2 NATIONAL CURRICULUM FRAMEWORK – GOVERNMENT FRAMEWORK

Working towards the expected standard

The pupil can:

- write for a range of purposes
- use paragraphs to organise ideas
- in narratives, describe settings and characters
- in non-narrative writing, use simple devices to structure the writing and support the reader (e.g. headings, sub-headings, bullet points)
- use capital letters, full stops, question marks, commas for lists, and apostrophes for contractions mostly correctly
- spell correctly most words from the year 3 / year 4 spelling list, and some words from the year 5 / year 6 spelling list
- write legibly

Working at the expected standard

The pupil can:

- write effectively for a range of purposes and audiences, selecting language that shows good awareness of the reader (e.g. the use of the first person in a diary; direct address in instructions and persuasive writing)
- in narratives, describe settings, characters, and atmosphere
- integrate dialogue in narratives to convey character and advance the action
- select vocabulary and grammatical structures that reflect what the writing requires, doing this mostly appropriately (e.g. using contracted forms in dialogues in narrative; using passive verbs to affect how information is presented; using modal verbs to suggest degrees of possibility)
- use a range of devices to build cohesion (e.g. conjunctions, adverbials of time and place, pronouns, synonyms) within and across paragraphs
- use verb tenses consistently and correctly throughout their writing
- use the range of punctuation taught at key stage 2 mostly correctly (e.g. inverted commas and other punctuation to indicate direct speech)
- spell correctly most words from the year 5 / year 6 spelling list, and use a dictionary to check the spelling of uncommon or more ambitious vocabulary
- maintain legibility in joined handwriting when writing at speed

Working at greater depth

The pupil can:

- write effectively for a range of purposes and audiences, selecting the appropriate form and drawing independently on what they have read as models for their own writing (e.g. literary language, characterisation, structure)
- distinguish between the language of speech and writing and choose the appropriate register
- exercise an assured and conscious control over levels of formality, particularly through manipulating grammar and vocabulary to achieve this
- use the range of punctuation taught at key stage 2 correctly (e.g. semicolons, dashes, colons, hyphens) and, when necessary, use such punctuation precisely to enhance meaning and avoid ambiguity.

MEET THE MRS WORDSMITH TEAM

Editor-in-Chief
Sofia Fenichell

Associate Creative Director
Lady San Pedro

Art Director
Craig Kellman

Writers

Tatiana Barnes

Mark Holland
Sawyer Eaton

Amelia Mehra

Researcher
Eleni Savva

Lexicographer
Ian Brookes

Designers

Suzanne Bullat
James Sales

Fabrice Gourdel
James Webb
Holly Jones

Caroline Henriksen
Jess Macadam

Producers
Eva Schumacher Payne
Leon Welters

Academic Advisors
Emma Madden
Prof. Susan Neuman

Project Managers
Senior Editor Helen Murray
Design Manager Sunita Gahir

Senior Production Editor Jennifer Murray
Senior Production Controller Louise Minihane
Publishing Director Mark Searle

DK Delhi
DTP Designers Satish Gaur and Rohit Rojal
Senior DTP Designer Pushpak Tyagi
Pre-production Manager Sunil Sharma
Managing Art Editor Romi Chakraborty

DK would like to thank Roohi Sehgal and Julia March
for editorial assistance.

First published in Great Britain in 2021 by
Dorling Kindersley Limited
A Penguin Random House Company
DK, One Embassy Gardens, 8 Viaduct Gardens,
London, SW11 7BW

The authorised representative in the EEA is
Dorling Kindersley Verlag GmbH. Arnulfstr. 124,
80636 Munich, Germany.

This content is also available to purchase as
a printable workbook at mrswordsmith.com

10 9 8 7 6 5 4 3 2
004–325950–August/2021

A CIP catalogue record for this book
is available from the British Library.
ISBN 978-0-24152-714-6

Printed and bound in the UK

www.dk.com

mrswordsmith.com

For the curious

This book was made with
Forest Stewardship Council™
certified paper – one small
step in DK's commitment to
a sustainable future.

The building blocks of reading

OUR JOB IS TO INCREASE YOUR CHILD'S READING AGE

READ TO LEARN

LEARN TO READ

Phonemic Awareness → Phonics → Fluency → Vocabulary → Reading Comprehension

READICULOUS

Readiculous App
App Store & Google Play

Word Tag App
App Store & Google Play

This book adheres to the science of reading. Our research-backed learning helps children progress through phonemic awareness, phonics, fluency, vocabulary, and reading comprehension.

How to Write a Story is dedicated to some of the main characters in the life of Mrs Wordsmith.

To our artists, designers, and writers, for making our ideas a reality. To our children, for giving us the only feedback that really matters. To Kurt Vonnegut, for inspiring us with his study of the anatomy of a story.

And to Emma Madden of Fox Primary School, for her tireless contributions to ensuring our work is useful for teachers and learners in the classroom.